MW00875089

The Insane But True

Basketball Trivia

Book

A Fun Collection of 700 Timeless Trivia
Quizzes To Satisfy The Curious Brains of
Die-Hard NBA Fans!

Curtice Mang, **History** Compacted

Copyright © 2022 by Sea Vision Publishing, LLC

All Rights Reserved.

No part of this publication may be reproduced, distributed, or transmitted in any form or by any means, including photocopying, recording, electronic or mechanical methods, without the prior written permission of the publisher, except in the case of brief quotations embodied in critical reviews and certain other non-commercial uses permitted by copyright law.

Much research, from a variety of sources, has gone into the compilation of this material. We strive to keep the information up-to-date to the best knowledge of the author and publisher; the materials contained herein is factually correct. Neither the publisher nor author will be held responsible for any inaccuracies. This publication is produced solely for informational purposes, and it is not intended to hurt or defame anyone involved.

ISBN: 9798849533759

Table of Contents

A Note

From History Compacted

Hi there!

This is Jason Chen, founder of History Compacted. Before you continue your journey to the past, I want to take a quick moment to explain our position on history and the purpose of our books.

To us, history is more than just facts, dates, and names. We see history as pieces of stories that led to the world we know today. Besides, it makes it much more fun seeing it that way too.

That is why History Compacted was created: to tell amazing stories of the past and hopefully inspire you to search for more. After all, history would be too big for any one book. But what each book can give you is a piece of the puzzle to help you get to that fuller picture.

Lastly, I want to acknowledge the fact that history is often told from different perspectives. Depending on the topic and your upbringing, you might agree or disagree with how we present the facts. I understand disagreements are inevitable. That is why with a team of diverse writers, we aim to tell each story from a more neutral perspective. I hope this note can help you better understand our position and goals.

Now without further ado, let your journey to the past begins!

Basketball Beginnings, NBA Origins, and Franchises

The origins of basketball date back to the late 19th century as an indoor means to keep energetic YMCA gym students physically active during the harsh winter months. From there it grew and expanded into high schools and colleges around the United States and eventually led to the creation of pro leagues. There were barnstorming pro teams and several leagues came and went before the National Basketball Association gained a foothold.

Today, basketball is a world-wide sport, played from French Lick, Indiana, to Shanghai, China, from San Martin, Argentina to Dijon, France. NBA teams are now valued in the billions as is the March Madness college tournament television contract.

1. The game of basketball was invented in what city?

   A. Cooperstown, New York

   B. Rochester, New York

   C. Springfield, Massachusetts

   D. Canton, Ohio

2. Who is the person credited with inventing basketball?

   A. James Naismith

   B. Abner Doubleday

   C. Abe Saperstein

   D. George Halas

3. In what year was basketball invented?

   A. 1890

   B. 1891

C. 1902

D. 1910

4. What were first used as basketball goals when the game was created?

    A. Cardboard boxes

    B. Apple crates

    C. Soccer goals

    D. Peach baskets

5. How high were the first basketball goals?

    A. 8 feet

    B. 10 feet

    C. 10.5 feet

    D. 12 feet

6. Originally, there were 13 rules. One rule determined the number of players each team could have on the court at one time. How many players per side were allowed?

A. Five

B. Six

C. Eight

D. Nine

7. The National Basketball League was the first professional basketball league. What year was it founded?

A. 1893

B. 1898

C. 1900

D. 1910

8. Some of the early professional teams weren't in leagues. Instead, they were barnstorming teams, traveling across the

country to take on all comers. Which of these teams was NOT one of the early barnstorming teams?

   A. Philadelphia SPHA's

   B. Original Celtics

   C. Bristol Pile Drivers

   D. New York Rens

9. Joe Lapchick and Nat Holman were stars of which early barnstorming team?

   A. Harlem Globetrotters

   B. New York Rens

   C. Original Celtics

   D. Philadelphia SPHA's

10. Who was the founder and owner of the Harlem Globetrotters?

   A. Goose Tatum

B. Abe Saperstein

C. Walter Kennedy

D. Maurice Podoloff

11. When were the Harlem Globetrotters founded?

A. 1926

B. 1928

C. 1930

D. 1933

12. True or False. Basketball teams and players were often referred to as cagers because the court often had to have chicken wire around the outside of the court to keep the rowdy fans from the players and referees.

13. What city hosted the very first NBA game on November 1, 1946?

A. New York City

B. Philadelphia

C. Boston

D. Toronto

14. Although now known as the National Basketball Association, the first three seasons, beginning in 1946-1947, what was the league called?

A. Basketball Association of America

B. Eastern Basketball League

C. Northern Basketball League

D. American Basketball League

15. True or False. The Basketball Association of America merged with the Midwest Basketball Association in 1949 and renamed the NBA.

16. What two teams played in the inaugural NBA game on November 1, 1946?

A. Toronto Raptors-New York Knicks

B. New York Knicks-Tri-Cities Blackhawks

C. Toronto Huskies-New York Knicks

D. Buffalo Bisons-Waterloo Hawks

17. Who scored the first points in NBA history?

A. Joe Lapchick

B. Oscar "Ossie" Schectman

C. Butch van Breda Kolff

D. Ed Sadowski

18. How many teams competed in the NBA's first season in 1946-1947?

   A. 17

   B. 14

   C. 15

   D. 11

19. One of these teams was not a franchise in the NBA in the 1946-1947 season.

   A. Providence Steamrollers

   B. St. Louis Bombers

   C. Chicago Stags

   D. Cleveland Rebels

20. True or False. The Boston Celtics were not an original NBA franchise in 1946-1947.

21. The Pistons franchise began in what city?

A. Detroit

B. Sheboygan

C. Fort Wayne

D. Pittsburgh

22. The Sacramento Kings franchise began in another city and under another name. What was the franchise originally called?

A. Syracuse Nationals

B. Tri-Cities Blackhawks

C. Rochester Royals

D. St. Louis Bombers

23. What other cities did the Kings franchise play in before arriving in Sacramento?

A. Cincinnati

B. Kansas City

C. Omaha

D. All of the above

24. What season did the New York Knicks begin play in the NBA?

A. 1946-1947

B. 1950-1951

C.

1952-1953

D. 1960-1961

25. True or False. The Providence Steamrollers were one of the original franchises to play in the 1946-1947 season.

26. How many teams were in the league when it started its second season in 1947-1948?

A. 16

B. 12

C. 10

D. 8

27. The Chicago Bulls began playing in what season NBA season?

A. 1963-1964

B. 1966-1967

C. 1968-1969

D. 1970-1971

28. The Bulls were not the first NBA franchise in Chicago. One of these teams was NOT a previous unsuccessful NBA team in Chicago.

A. Chicago Stags

B. Chicago Staleys

C. Chicago Packers

D. Chicago Zephyrs

29. The Philadelphia 76ers franchise began play in another city and under another name. Name the city and team name.

A. Chicago Stags

B. Washington Capitols

C. Syracuse Nationals

D. New York Rens

30. In 1971, the NBA expanded by adding three teams. Which of these teams was NOT an expansion team that year?

A. Buffalo Braves

B. Cleveland Cavaliers

C. Portland Trailblazers

D. St. Louis Bombers

31. The Lakers franchise began in what city?

A. St. Paul

B. Minneapolis

C. Milwaukee

D. Syracuse

32. In what season did the Lakers first play in Los Angeles?

A. 1958-1959

B. 1959-1960

C. 1960-1961

D. 1965-1966

33. Baltimore had a franchise in the NBA from 1947-1954. What was the team name?

A. Capitols

B. Presidents

C. Bullets

D. Senators

34. What year did the Pistons franchise first play in the NBA?

A. 1948-1949

B. 1949-1950

C. 1952-1953

D. 1955-1956

35. True or False. The Sheboygan Redskins was never a franchise in the NBA.

36. The Washington Wizards have gone under other names in other cities. Which of these were other names of the franchise?

A. Baltimore Bullets

B. Capitol Bullets

C. Chicago Zephyrs

D. All of the above

37. The Rockets were an expansion franchise for the 1967-1968 season. In what city did the franchise begin?

A. El Cajon

B. San Diego

C. San Francisco

D. San Antonio

38. Prior to Atlanta, the Hawks played in St. Louis. What was the team's first season in Atlanta?

A. 1967-1968

B. 1968-1969

C. 1969-1970

D. 1972-1973

39. Even before playing in St. Louis, the Hawks played in yet another city for four seasons. Name the city.

A. Denver

B. Little Rock

C. Milwaukee

D. Hartford

40. What year did the Seattle Supersonics begin NBA play as an expansion team?

A. 1964-1965

B. 1966-1967

C. 1967-1968

D. 1968-1969

41. What is the franchise that began as the Seattle Supersonics now called?

A. Miami Heat

B. Los Angeles Clippers

C. Utah Jazz

D. Oklahoma City Thunder

42. The Warriors franchise has played in three different cities. Which one of these cities has not been a home of the Warriors?

A. San Francisco

B. Oakland

C. Santa Clara

D. Philadelphia

43. True of False. The Milwaukee Bucks entered the NBA in 1968.

44. Follow-up question. In what season did the Bucks win their first NBA championship?

A. 1969-1970

B. 1970-1971

C. 1973-1974

D. 1980-1981

45. For the 1978-1979 season the Buffalo Braves relocated to a new city and changed the team name. What was the new city and name?

A. Dallas Chapparals

B. San Diego Conquistadors

C. San Diego Clippers

D. Washington Generals

46. The Phoenix Suns joined the NBA as an expansion team in what year?

A. 1968

B. 1969

C. 1971

D. 1975

47. The Jazz franchise was an expansion NBA team in what year?

A. 1970

B. 1972

C. 1974

D. 1975

48. In what city did the Jazz originally play in?

A. Jackson

B. Birmingham

C. New Orleans

D. Atlanta

49. The Grizzlies now play in Memphis. What city did they originally play in?

A. Seattle

B. Portland

C. Vancouver

D. Fort Wayne

50. True or False. Indianapolis once had a franchise in the NBA called the Olympians.

51. The NBA merged with the ABA for the 1976-1977 season. Four ABA teams joined the NBA for the start of that season. One of these teams did not join the NBA as part of the merger.

A. Denver Nuggets

B. San Antonio Spurs

C. Indiana Pacers

D. Carolina Cougars

52. The Miami Heat was an expansion team for the 1988-1989 season. What division did the team originally play in?

A. Atlantic

B. Central

C. Midwest

D. Pacific

53. One other team joined the NBA as an expansion team for the 1988-1989 season. Name the team.

A. Charlotte Hornets

B. Memphis Tams

C. Miami Floridians

D. Buffalo Bison

54. The Dallas Mavericks joined the NBA as an expansion team in what year?

A. 1976

B. 1978

C. 1980

D. 1985

55. After having a team in the early years of the league that eventually relocated, Minneapolis, Minnesota, finally got an expansion franchise in what year?

A. 1985

B. 1988

C. 1989

D. 1992

56. What is the name of the Minnesota franchise?

A. Twins

B. Timberwolves

C. Tundras

D. Devils

57. What was the Orlando Magic's first NBA season?

A. 1989-1990

B. 1992-1993

C. 1995-1996

D. 2000-2001

58. Only three teams remain from the inaugural 1946-1947 NBA season. One of these teams did not play in the first NBA season.

A. Celtics

B. Knicks

C. Lakers

D. Warriors

59. The city of Toronto had a franchise in the first NBA season, but it folded after the season's end. The NBA finally awarded Toronto an expansion franchise in what year?

A. 1991

B. 1992

C. 1995

D. 1997

60. Which team is considered the first dynasty of the NBA?

A. Boston Celtics

B. Minneapolis Lakers

C. Philadelphia Warriors

D. New York Knicks

61. New York is known as the Knicks, but that is an abbreviation of the full name. What is the official name of the New York team?

A. Knickerbockers

B. Knick-knacks

C. Knickers

D. Knicklebacks

62. Who was the first draft pick of the Tri-City Blackhawks in 1950?

A. Johnny Kerr

B. Bob Cousy

C. Vern Mikkelsen

D. Bob Pettit

63. The Chicago Packers were the first NBA expansion team in 1961. One of the players selected in the expansion

draft would later become the long-time coach of the Indiana Pacers. Name the player.

A. Dave Budd

B. Gene Conley

C. Bobby "Slick" Leonard

D. Jerry Sloan

64. The next NBA expansion draft featured the subsequent Chicago franchise—the Bulls. One of the players chosen in that expansion draft would coach the team in its inaugural season. Name the player.

A. Johnny "Red" Kerr

B. Al Bianchi

C. Dick Motta

D. Norm Van Lier

65. This player has the ignominious distinction of being selected by expansion teams in three expansion drafts covering multiple years. Who was this player?

A. Len Chappell

B. George Wilson

C. John McGlocklin

D. Nate Bowman

66. The Nets franchise has played in multiple cities in and around the New York area. The team was never known as one of these names.

A. New York Nets

B. Brooklyn Nets

C. New Jersey Nets

D. Staten Island Nets

67. The Charlotte Hornets relocated to this city beginning with the 2002-2003 season.

A. St. Louis

B. New Orleans

C. Memphis

D. Portland

68. What is the name of the New Orleans franchise now?

A. Billikens

B. Jazz

C. Pelicans

D. Levies

69. For the 2004-2005 season, the NBA awarded Charlotte another franchise. What was the name of the team when it joined the league?

A. Wildcats

B. Huskies

C. Bees

D. Bobcats

70. Beginning in 2014, the Charlotte team changed the name of the franchise. What was it changed to?

A. Hornets

B. Stingrays

C. Blackhawks

D. Tar Heels

71. Dating back even before the birth of the NBA, which team is the oldest continuously operating team in the NBA?

A. Celtics

B. Hawks

C. Knicks

D. Kings

72. Several cities have had multiple NBA franchises (at separate times). One of these cities never had two separate franchises.

A. Minneapolis

B. Chicago

C. Detroit

D. Philadelphia

73. In addition to being head coach of the Boston Celtics for 16 seasons, he was also general manager for 34 years.

A. Danny Ainge

B. Arnold "Red" Auerbach

C. K.C. Jones

D. Tom Heinsohn

74. The owner of the Syracuse Nationals was responsible for developing the idea for the 24-second shot clock.

A. Al Bianchi

B. Ben Kerner

C. Daniel Biasone

D. Dolph Schayes

75. When did he NBA adopt the 24-second shot clock?

A. 1950-1951

B. 1954-1955

C. 1956-1957

D. 1959-1960

76. Jerry Colangelo became general manager of this franchise in 1968 and later became the principal owner.

A. Phoenix Suns

B. Milwaukee Bucks

C. Philadelphia 76ers

D. New York Knicks

77. As general manager, this individual was the architect of the great Chicago Bulls teams of the 1990s.

A. Billy McKinney

B. Jerry Krause

C. Mitch Kupchak

D. Louis Mohs

78. He was the first African-American to be hired as a general manager of an NBA franchise and has had a career as a team executive that spans nearly 50 years.

A. Joe Dumars

B. Elgin Baylor

C. Wayne Embry

D. Bob Lanier

79. This individual served as general manager/executive for the Chicago Bulls, Atlanta Hawks, Philadelphia 76ers, and Orlando Magic in his 51 years in the NBA.

A. Jerry West

B. Billy Knight

C. Pat Williams

D. Don Nelson

80. He holds the distinction of being the longest tenured general manager in the history of the Hawks franchise.

A. Pete Babcock

B. Marty Blake

C. Pat Williams

D. David Stern

81. Since the inception of the league in 1946, how many commissioners has the NBA had?

A. 12

B. 10

C. 8

D. 5

82. Who was the first NBA commissioner?

A. Ed Gottlieb

B. Walter Kennedy

C. Maurice Podoloff

D. Walter Brown

83. The NBA championship trophy is named for this commissioner.

A. Larry O'Brien

B. Walter Kennedy

C. Maurice Podoloff

D. David Stern

84. Through the 2020-2021 season, which franchise has the highest all-time NBA winning percentage, regular season and playoffs?

A. Boston Celtics

B. Los Angeles Lakers

C. Utah Jazz

D. San Antonio Spurs

85. Through the 2020-2021 season, which franchise has the lowest all-time NBA winning percentage, regular season and playoffs?

A. Los Angeles Clippers

B. Minnesota Timberwolves

C. Sacramento Kings

D. Memphis Grizzlies

86. What team has played the most regular season games in NBA history?

A. Boston Celtics

B. New York Knicks

C. Golden State Warriors

D. Detroit Pistons

87. In 1971-1972, the Los Angeles Lakers set the all-time record for consecutive regular season wins. How many consecutive games did the Lakers win?

A. 20

B. 25

C. 30

D. 33

88. Since the advent of the 24-second shot clock, which team has the highest season scoring average?

A. 1981-1982 Denver Nuggets

B. 1961-1962 Philadelphia Warriors

C. 1966-1967 Philadelphia 76ers

D. 1982-1983 Denver Nuggets

89. Since the advent of the 24-second shot clock, which team has the lowest season scoring average?

A. 2002-2003 Denver Nuggets

B. 1954-1955 Milwaukee Hawks

C. 1998-1999 Chicago Bulls

D. 1999-2000 Chicago Bulls

90. On November 22, 1950, the Fort Wayne Pistons and the Minneapolis Lakers played the lowest scoring game in NBA history. What was the final score?

A. 19-18

B. 25-24

C. 33-30

D. 35-34

91. One player from the lowest scoring NBA game had 15 of his team's points. Name the player.

A. Vern Mikkelsen

B. Slater Martin

C. George Mikan

D. Larry Foust

92. On December 13, 1983, the Detroit Pistons and Denver Nuggets played in the highest scoring game in NBA history. What was the final score?

A. 173-143

B. 169-147

C. 171-166

D. 186-184

93. Who was the leading scorer in the highest scoring game?

A. Kiki Vanderweghe

B. Alex English

C. Isiah Thomas

D. Kelly Tripuka

94. True or False. The Phoenix Suns hold the record for most points scored in one half with 107.

95. The Golden State Warriors set an all-time record for most regular season wins during the 2015-2016 season. What was the Warriors record that season?

A. 69-13

B. 70-12

C. 72-10

D. 73-9

96. Prior to the 2015-2016 Warriors, the 1995-1996 Bulls had the best single-season record. What was the Bulls record that season?

A. 68-13

B. 69-13

C. 70-12

D. 72-10

97. What team holds the record for the fewest wins during an 82-game regular season?

A. Charlotte Hornets

B. Philadelphia 76ers

C. Dallas Mavericks

D. Cleveland Cavaliers

98. The Portland Trailblazers have had the first pick in the NBA draft on four separate occasions. Which one of these players was not a first pick in the draft by the Trailblazers?

A. Bill Walton

B. LaRue Martin

C. Clyde Drexler

D. Greg Oden

99. What team(s) has the record for the best home single season record?

A. San Antonio Spurs

B. Chicago Bulls

C. Boston Celtics

D. A and C

100. The 1984 NBA draft is considered one of the best draft classes of all-time. Hakeem Olajuwon was the first pick in the draft and Michael Jordon was the third pick. Who was picked with the second pick in the draft?

A. Charles Barkley

B. Otis Thorpe

C. John Stockton

D. Sam Bowie

101. In 1959, the Philadelphia Warriors selected this player with their "territorial" pick in the first round of the NBA draft.

A. Nate Thurmond

B. Wilt Chamberlain

C. Dolph Schayes

D. Billy Cunningham

102. In 1960, the Cincinnati Royals selected this player with their "territorial" pick in the first round of the NBA draft.

A. Oscar Robertson

B. Connie Dierking

C. Bob Boozer

D. Jack Twyman

103. The Cleveland Cavaliers selected LeBron James with what pick in the 2003 NBA draft?

A. First

B. Fourth

C. Sixth

D. Tenth

104. In 1969, these two teams flipped a coin to see who would get the first pick in the NBA draft and select Lew Alcindor (later Kareem Abdul-Jabbar).

A. Phoenix/Milwaukee

B. Milwaukee/Seattle

C. Los Angeles/Milwaukee

D. Los Angeles/San Diego

105. Which team is considered the first dynasty of the NBA beginning with the 1951-1952 season?

A. Detroit Pistons

B. Minneapolis Lakers

C. Boston Celtics

D. Syracuse Nationals

106. Which team drafted Bill Russell in 1956 NBA draft?

A. Boston Celtics

B. St. Louis Hawks

C. Cincinnati Royals

D. Syracuse Nationals

107. The Cleveland Cavaliers had the first pick in the NBA draft in 2013 and 2014. Which players did they select?

A. Anthony Davis/Andrew Wiggins

B. Andrew Wiggins/Karl Anthony-Towns

C. Anthony Bennett/Andrew Wiggins

D. Anthony Bennett/Anthony Davis

108. Through the 2020-2021 season, what team holds the record for most 3-point shots made per game in a season?

A. Utah Jazz

B. Houston Rockets

C. Milwaukee Bucks

D. Portland Trailblazers

109. When was the 3-point shot first introduced in the NBA?

A. 1975-1976

B. 1977-1978

C. 1979-1980

D. 1983-1984

110. What player is credited with making the first 3-pointer in NBA history?

A. Kevin Grevey

B. Larry Bird

C. Chris Ford

D. Fred Brown

111. True or False. Stephen Curry was the first player in NBA history to make 3,000 3-point shots in a career.

112. Rick Barry was one of the best free throw shooters in the history of the game. What was unique about his free throw shooting style?

A. He stood three feet behind the foul line

B. He shot underhanded

C. He shot with one hand behind his back

D. He closed one eye

113. Name the player who also had an unusual free throw shooting style—he shot a jump shot.

A. LeBron James

B. James Harden

C. Doug Collins

D. Hal Greer

114. This team holds the record for the highest field goal percentage in a season, set in 1984-1985.

A. Los Angeles Lakers

B. Chicago Bulls

C. Indiana Pacers

D. Houston Rockets

115. This team set a league record for the lowest field goal percentage in a season, set in 1954-1955.

A. Milwaukee Bucks

B. St. Louis Hawks

C. Milwaukee Hawks

D. Atlanta Hawks

116. In what season did the NBA first start including blocks and steals as official statistical categories?

A. 1966-1967

B. 1970-1971

C. 1973-1974

D. 1980-1981

117. The Los Angeles Lakers used a territorial draft pick to select this UCLA guard in the 1964 NBA draft.

A. Walt Hazzard

B. Mike Warren

C. Jerry West

D. Tom Hawkins

118. The second NBA dynasty dominated the league from the mid-1950s through the end of the 1960s. Name the team.

A. Los Angeles Lakers

B. Philadelphia Warriors

C. Boston Celtics

D. New York Knicks

119. The Los Angeles Lakers selected another guard from UCLA with a "territorial" pick in the 1965 NBA draft. Who was he?

A. Rod Hundley

B. Tom Hawkins

C. Gail Goodrich

D. Pat Riley

120. What team was considered the NBA dynasty of the 1990s?

A. Detroit Pistons

B. Chicago Bulls

C. Los Angeles Lakers

D. Miami Heat

121. Who is the all-time leading scorer in the history of the Warriors franchise?

A. Wilt Chamberlain

B. Rick Barry

C. Paul Arizin

D. Stephen Curry

122. Who is the all-time leading rebounder for the Phoenix Suns?

A. Amare Stoudemire

B. Alvan Adams

C. Charles Barkley

D. Tom Chambers

123. Who has played more games for the Portland Trailblazers than any other player?

A. Damian Lillard

B. Clyde Drexler

C. Terry Porter

D. Cliff Robinson

124. Name the player with the most career assists for the New Orleans Pelicans franchise.

A. Baron Davis

B. Jrue Holiday

C. Chris Paul

D. Lonzo Ball

125. Who is the all-time leading rebounder for the Hawks franchise?

A. Tree Rollins

B. Paul Silas

C. Bob Pettit

D. Zelmo Beatty

Answers

1. Basketball was first invented and played in Springfield, Massachusetts.

2. Dr. James Naismith, then working for the YMCA invented the rules for basketball as an indoor "athletic distraction" during the cold New England winter months.

3. Naismith invented this new game in 1890.

4. The first goals were peach baskets nailed to the wall.

5. The first peach basket basketball goals were 10 feet high, just at the height the goals remain today.

6. Naismith's original rules allowed for nine players per side.

7. The first professional league, the National Basketball League, began play in 1898. It disbanded in 1904.

8. The Bristol Pile Drivers team was a member of the National Basketball League.

9. Joe Lapchick and Nat Holman played for the Original Celtics.

10. Abe Saperstein was the founder and owner of the Harlem Globetrotters.

11. Saperstein founded the Globetrotters in 1926.

12. True. Chicken wire and other fencing was often erected around the basketball court to keep players, coaches, and referees safe from unruly fans and the objects they may attempt to hurl onto the court.

13. Toronto hosted the very first National Basketball Association game.

14. The original name of the league was the Basketball Association of America (BAA).

15. False. The Basketball Association of America merged with the National Basketball League, which began play in 1937, in 1949, and was rebranded the National Basketball Association.

16. The New York Knicks battled the Toronto Huskies in the very first game in NBA history (then the BAA).

17. Oscar "Ossie" Schectman of the Knicks scored the first points in NBA history on a two-handed scoop shot.

18. There were 11 NBA teams for the first NBA season in 1946-1947.

19. The Chicago Stags were one of the original NBA franchises.

20. False. The Boston Celtics were one of the original 11 NBA teams.

21. The Pistons franchise began play as the Fort Wayne Zollner Pistons in the NBL. They were named after owner and founder Fred Zollner, who was an automobile piston magnate.

22. The Sacramento Kings franchise started out as the Rochester Royals.

23. The Rochester Royals relocated first to Cincinnati. The franchise later moved again to Kansas City and Omaha, splitting home games between the two cities for three seasons. They played exclusively in Kansas City before moving again to Sacramento for the 1985-1986 season.

24. The New York Knicks began play in 1946-1947 as one of the original NBA franchises.

25. True. The Providence Steamrollers were an original NBA franchise in 1946-1947.

26. The second NBA season in 1947-1948 had only eight franchises, losing three from the inaugural season.

27. The Chicago Bulls were an expansion team for the 1966-1967 season.

28. The Chicago Staleys were never a franchise in the NBA.

29. For the 1963-1964 season, the Syracuse National relocated to Philadelphia to become the 76ers.

30. The St. Louis Bombers were not one of the 1971-1972 NBA expansion teams.

31. The Lakers began in Minneapolis.

32. The Lakers first played in Los Angeles with the 1960-1961 season.

33. The original NBA franchise in Baltimore was called the Bullets. The team played beginning with the 1947-1948 season until the team was disbanded in November1954.

34. The Fort Wayne Pistons joined the NBA for the 1948-1949 season.

35. False. The Sheboygan Redskins played one season in the NBA, 1949-1950, finishing with a 22-40 record.

36. The Washington Wizards at one time or another went by all of those names—Baltimore Bullets, Capitol Bullets, Chicago Zephyrs.

37. The Rockets franchise began in San Diego.

38. The Hawks began playing in Atlanta for the 1968-1969 season.

39. The Hawks started in Milwaukee for the 1951-1952 season.

40. The expansion Seattle Supersonics began their inaugural NBA season in 1967-1968.

41. The Supersonics moved to Oklahoma City in 2008-2009, changing the team name to the Thunder in the process.

42. The Warriors have played in Philadelphia, Oakland, and San Francisco (twice), but never in Santa Clara.

43. True. The Bucks began play in the 1968-1969 season.

44. The Bucks won the NBA championship in 1970-1971, only the team's third season.

45. The Buffalo Braves moved to San Diego to become the Clippers.

46. The Suns were an expansion team in the 1968-1969 season.

47. The Jazz began NBA play as an expansion team in 1974-1975.

48. The Jazz franchise began in New Orleans.

49. The Grizzlies franchise began in Vancouver.

50. True. The Indianapolis Olympians began play in the NBA in 1949 before folding in 1953.

51. The Carolina Cougars were not one of the ABA franchises to join the NBA for the 1976-1977 season.

52. The Miami Heat played their first NBA season in the Midwest Division before moving to the Atlantic Division the following season.

53. The Charlotte Hornets were another expansion team in 1988-1989.

54. The Dallas began NBA play in the 1980-1981 season.

55. Minnesota was an expansion team for the 1989-1990 season.

56. The Minnesota team is called the Timberwolves.

57. 1989-1990 was the first season of play for the Orlando Magic.

58. The Lakers were not an original NBA franchise, beginning play in 1948-1949.

59. The Toronto Raptors began play in the 1955-1996 season.

60. The Minneapolis Lakers were the first NBA dynasty, winning five NBA championships from 1948-1949 through 1953-1954.

61. The New York franchise is officially called the Knickerbockers.

62. Bob Cousy was drafted in the first round by the Tri-City Blackhawks in 1950. However, he was traded to the Chicago Stags one month later. The Chicago franchise folded before the season began. Cousy was chosen by the Boston Celtics in the Chicago Stags dispersal draft. Cousy never played for the Blackhawks or the Stags.

63. Bobby "Slick" Leonard played for Chicago Packers in their inaugural season and was the second leading scorer with 16.1 points per game. He would become the long-time and very successful coach of the Indiana Pacers in both the ABA and NBA,

64. Johnny "Red" Kerr coached the Bulls in their first NBA season, finishing with a 33-48 regular season record.

65. Len Chappell was selected by the Bulls in the 1966 expansion draft, the Milwaukee Bucks in the 1968 expansion draft, and the Cleveland Cavaliers in the 1970 expansion draft.

66. The Nets franchise was never known as the Staten Island Nets.

67. The Charlotte Hornets moved the franchise to New Orleans prior to the 2002-2003 season

68. The current New Orleans team is known as the Pelicans.

69. The new franchise in Charlotte beginning in the 2004-2005 season was the Bobcats.

70. The Charlotte franchise reclaimed the name Hornets beginning with the 2014-2015 season.

71. Believe it or not, the Kings franchise is the oldest continuously run franchise, beginning play in 1923 as a semi-pro team. They have operated in some form or another ever since joining the NBA for the 1948-1949 season.

72. The only NBA franchise Detroit has ever had has been the Pistons.

73. Arnold "Red" Auerbach served as coach and general manager for 16 seasons and then just general manager of the Boston Celtics after that.

74. Syracuse Nationals owner Daniel Biasone created the 24-second shot clock as a means of speeding up the game.

75. The NBA adopted the 24-second shot clock for the 1954-1955 season.

76. Jerry Colangelo became the general manager of the Phoenix Suns in 1968.

77. Jerry Krause was the general manager largely responsible for building the Chicago Bulls teams of the 1990s.

78. After playing 11 seasons in the NBA, Wayne Embry became the first African-American general manager in the league when he was hired by the Milwaukee Bucks in 1971.

79. Pat Williams served as general manager for the Bulls, Hawks, 76ers, and Magic during his lengthy NBA management career.

80. Pete Babcock is the longest-tenured general manager in Hawks history, holding that position from 1990-2003.

81. There have been five NBA commissioners since the inception of the NBA.

82. Maurice Podoloff was the first NBA commissioner, serving from 1946-1963.

83. The NBA championship trophy is named after Larry O'Brien, the league's third commissioner.

84. The San Antonio Spurs have the best all-time team winning percentage of .613.

85. The Minnesota Timberwolves have the lowest all-time winning percentage at .394.

86. Through the 2020-2021 season, the Boston Celtics played the most games in league history with 5,902 games.

87. The 1971-1972 Los Angeles Lakers won 33 games in a row that year, finishing with a 69-13 record.

88. The 1981-1982 Denver Nuggets averaged an all-time best 126.5 points per game.

89. The 1998-1999 Chicago Bulls average only 91.9 points per game, the lowest average since the advent of the shot clock.

90. The Pistons beat the Lakers 19-18 in the lowest scoring game in NBA history.

91. George Mikan scored 18 of the Lakers 18 points.

92. The Pistons beat the Nuggets 186-184.

93. Kiki Vandeweghe scored 51 points of the Nuggets 184 points/

94. True. The Phoenix Suns scored 107 points in the first half on November 10, 1990, as they defeated the Denver Nuggets 173-143.

95. The 2015-2016 Golden State Warriors finished with a 73-9 regular season record.

96. The 1995-1996 Bulls had a 72-10 regular season record.

97. The 1972-1973 Philadelphia 76ers had a woeful 9-73 record that season.

98. The Portland Trailblazers drafter Clyde Drexler with the 14th pick in the first round of 1983 NBA draft.

99. The 1985-1986 Boston Celtics and the 2015-2016 San Antonio Spurs both finished the regular season with a 40-1 home record.

100. The Portland Trailblazers drafted Sam Bowie with the second pick in the 1984 NBA draft, passing on Michael Jordon.

101. Wilt Chamberlain, who played college ball at Kansas, but played in high school at Overbrook High School in Philadelphia, was selected by the Warriors with their "territorial" draft pick in 1959.

102. The Cincinnati Royals drafted Oscar Robertson, from Ohio State, with their "territorial" pick in the 1960 draft.

103. Lebron James was selected with the first pick of the 2003 NBA draft by the Cleveland Cavaliers.

104. Following the 1968-1969 season the Phoenix Suns and Milwaukee Bucks flipped a coin to see who would get the first pick in the draft. The Suns called heads and it came up tails.

105. The Minneapolis Lakers were the league's first dynasty, winning five titles between 1948-1949 and 1953-1954.

106. The St. Louis Hawks drafted Bill Russell with the second pick in the 1956 NBA draft. He was subsequently traded to Boston on the same day.

107. The Cleveland Cavaliers selected Anthony Bennett with the first pick in the 2013 draft followed by Andrew Wiggins in the first round of the 2014 draft.

108. The Utah Jazz set a single season record for 3-point shots made per game with an average of 16.7.

109. The NBA adopted the 3-point shot with the 1979-1980.

110. Kevin Grevey of the Washington Bullets is credited with making the first 3-point shot in history in 1979.

111. True. Stephen Curry is the first player in NBA history to make 3,000 3-point shots.

112. Rick Barry shot his free throws underhanded. He was a career .900 free throw shooter.

113. Hal Greer shot a jump shot for his free throws. He was a career .812 free throw shooter.

114. The 1984-1985 Los Angeles Lakers had an all-time best .545 field goal percentage for the season.

115. The 1954-1955 Milwaukee Hawks had an all-time NBA-worst field goal percentage of .362.

116. The NBA started including blocks and steals as official statistical categories for the 1973-1974 season.

117. The Lakers selected former Bruin Walt Hazzard in the 1964 draft.

118. The Boston Celtics dominated the NBA from 1957 through 1969, winning 11 championships in 13 years.

119. The Lakers selected former UCLA guard Gail Goodrich in the 1965 draft.

120. The Chicago Bulls won six NBA titles in the 1990s.

121. Stephen Curry is the Warriors franchise all-time leading scorer with 20,006 through the 2020-2021-season.

122. Alvan Adams, who played his entire career with the Phoenix Suns, is the team's all-time leading rebounder with 9,937 total rebounds.

123. Clyde Drexler played 867 games for the Portland Trailblazers, more than any other player.

124. Chris Paul is the New Orleans Pelicans franchise leader with 4,228 assists.

125. Bob Pettit is the all-time leading rebounder for the Hawks franchise with 12,849 total rebounds.

Players

While the game may have changed, one thing has been constant—there have always been great players. Each era has its own set of exceptionally talented players. In the early days of the NBA, it was led by standouts Mikan and Cousy, then Russell and Wilt, followed by Magic and Bird, then along came Jordon and James.

How do we determine what makes a great player? Is it their own talent, skill, and ability, or is it their worth to their team? Or both? Who is the best of their era or the best of all time? Those debates rage on and, most likely, will never be completely settled.

1. This Los Angeles Lakers great poured in 81 points in one game against the Toronto Raptors in 2006.

   A. Magic Johnson

   B. Shaquille O'Neal

   C. Kobe Bryant

   D. James Worthy

2. He is considered the first dominant player in the NBA. Who was he?

   A. Bob Pettit

   B. Slater Martin

   C. George Mikan

   D. Vern Mikkelsen

3.
Tim Duncan was given this nickname during his playing career with the San Antonio Spurs.

A. The Big Unit

B. The Big Spur

C. The Big Fundamental

D. The Big Guy

4.
True or False. John Stockton of the Utah Jazz is the NBA's all-time leader in assists.

5.
How many times did Michael Jordon lead the NBA in scoring average?

A. 7

B. 8

C. 9

D. 10

6. Giannis Antetokounmpo was selected by the Milwaukee Bucks with what pick in the first round of the 2013 NBA draft?

A. First

B. Fifth

C. Tenth

D. Fifteenth

7. Bob Pettit played from 1954-1965 for one franchise. Which team did he play his entire career for?

A. Bulls

B. Hawks

C. Warriors

D. Knicks

8. Isiah Thomas starred for 13 seasons in the NBA, all with the Detroit Pistons. How many times did he play in the NBA All-Star game?

A. 8

B. 10

C. 12

D. 13

9. Stephen Curry and Klay Thompson formed a dynamic backcourt for the Golden State Warriors. What was the nickname of the backcourt duo?

A. Splash Brothers

B. The Shooters

C. Score Brothers

D. Warrior Guardians

10. On March 2, 1962, Wilt Chamberlain scored 100 points against the New York Knicks, while playing for the Philadelphia Warriors. Where was the game played?

A. Hershey, PA

B. New York City, NY

C. Philadelphia, PA

D. Syracuse, NY

11. During his 100-point game, Chamberlain, a notoriously poor free throw shooter, shot 32 free throws. How any did he make.?

A. 16

B. 18

C. 24

D. 28

12. This player was known as "Dr. J."

A. Jerry Lucas

B. John Havlicek

C. Julius Erving

D. Joe Caldwell

13. Kevin Durant was a rookie in 2007-2008. What team did he play for in his rookie season?

A. Oklahoma City Thunder

B. Seattle Supersonics

C. Golden State Warriors

D. Portland Trailblazers

14. He was a member of the two New York Knick championships and was known as "Dollar Bill."

A. Bill Cartwright

B. Bill Bradley

C. Bill Hosket

D. Phil Jackson

15. True or False. Mark Price, who spent most of his 12-year career with the Cleveland Cavaliers, has a career free throw percentage of over 90%?

16. Who is the shortest player ever to play in the NBA?

A. Spud Webb

B. Slater Martin

C. Tyrone "Muggsy" Bogues

D. Nate "Tiny" Archibald

17. After being banned by the NBA for alleged point shaving in college and toiling with the Harlem Globetrotters, in the ABL and ABA, Connie Hawkins finally got a chance to play with this NBA team for the 1969-1970 season.

A. Los Angeles Lakers

B. Atlanta Hawks

C. Seattle Supersonics

D. Phoenix Suns

18. In 1980, the Los Angeles Lakers traded Don Ford and a 1980 first round draft pick to the Cleveland Cavaliers for Butch Lee and a 1982 first round draft pick. Who did the Lakers select with the draft pick from Cleveland in 1982?

A. Byron Scott

B. Kurt Rambis

C. James Worthy

D. Michael Cooper

19. How many times did Magic Johnson win the NBA MVP award?

A. 0

B. 2

C. 3

D. 5

20. While playing for the Denver Nuggets, this player led the league for three straight seasons, from 1993-1996, in blocked shots.

A. Dan Issel

B. Dikembe Mutombo

C. Alex English

D. Wayne Cooper

21. Kareem Abdul-Jabbar was named NBA MVP how many times?

A. Four

B. Five

C. Six

D. Nine

22. This player played for the Rockets and Bullets during his 16-year NBA career and was known as the "Big E."

A. Elmore Smith

B. Elvin Hayes

C. Elgin Baylor

D. Ed Sadowski

23. Through the 2020-2021 season, this player has averaged at least 25 points, five rebounds, and five assists in 15 different seasons, more than any other player in history.

A. Oscar Robertson

B. Russell Westbrook

C. Lebron James

D. Michael Jordon

24. This player is the all-time Miami Heat leader in points, assists, and steals.

A. Dwayne Wade

B. Chris Bosh

C. Lebron James

D. Glen Rice

25. Jerry West of the Los Angeles Lakers earned this nickname during his playing career.

A. Mr. Clutch

B. Mr. Laker

C. Mr. Mister

D. Mr. Big Shot

26. This former Philadelphia 76er holds the dubious record for most fouls in one season with 386. Name the player.

A. Shawn Kemp

B. Bill Robinzine

C. Darryl Dawkins

D. Lonnie Shelton

27. New York Knicks great Walt Frazier was given this nickname.

A. Clyde

B. The Flash

C. Mr. Defense

D. Man of Steal

28. Known as a rugged rebounder, Paul Silas played for five NBA teams. One of these teams is NOT a team Silas played for.

A. Atlanta Hawks

B. Phoenix Suns

C. San Diego Clippers

D. Boston Celtics

29. What is the NBA record for most assists in one game?

A. 25

B. 27

C. 28

D. 30

30. Patrick Ewing played 15 of his 17 seasons with the New York Knicks. How many times did he average over 20 points per game while playing for the Knicks?

A. 8

B. 10

C. 12

D. 13

31. This 1977-1978 MVP missed four full seasons due to foot injuries during his 14-year NBA career with the Trailblazers, Clippers, and Celtics.

A. Maurice Lucas

B. Mychal Thompson

C. Bill Walton

D. Swen Nater

32. This player was a two-time MVP during his second stint with the Phoenix Suns, leading their "seven seconds or less" fast break offense.

A. Amare Stoudemire

B. Steve Nash

C. Kevin Johnson

D. Eddie Johnson

33. Larry Bird played for the Boston Celtics from 1979-1992. How many times was he named MVP?

A. 1

B. 2

C. 3

D. 6

34. Representing the Cincinnati Royals in 1966, this guard is the unlikeliest All-Star game MVP.

A. Baily Howell

B. Sam Jones

C. Adrian Smith

D. Zelmo Betty

35. He was Bill Russell's teammate at the University of San Francisco and the Boston Celtics.

A. Sam Jones

B. K.C. Jones

C. Don Nelson

D. Bill Sharman

36. He was known by the nickname "The Pearl."

  A. Earl Williams

  B. Earl Lloyd

  C. Earl Watson

  D. Earl Monroe

37. Who was the first African American to play in the NBA?

  A. Earl Lloyd

  B. Chuck Cooper

  C. Nat Clifton

  D. Bill Russell

38. This LSU star came into the league in 1970-1971 with the Atlanta Hawks and was later traded to New Orleans Jazz.

A. Rich Kelley

B. Lou Hudson

C. Pete Maravich

D. Bob Pettit

39. True or False. Phil Jackson never won an NBA championship as a player.

40. Gary Payton was known as a tough defender during his 17-year career, primarily with the Seattle Supersonics. What was his nickname?

A. G-Pay

B. The Glove

C. The Pay-Man

D. The Stopper

41. Elgin Baylor played his entire career for this franchise?

A. Celtics

B. Lakers

C. Hawks

D. Warriors

42. He is recognized as the greatest European-born player to play in the NBA.

A. Detlef Schrempf

B. Arvydas Sabonis

C. Dirk Nowitzki

D. Domantas Sabonis

43. The NBA logo features a silhouette of which player?

A. Jerry West

B. Oscar Robertson

C. Bob Cousy

D. Elgin Baylor

44. He starred for both the University of Houston and the Houston Rockets and was known by the nickname "The Dream."

A. Hakeem Olajuwon

B. Calvin Murphy

C. Rudy Tomjanovich

D. James Harden

45. For the 1968-1969 season, this player was named both NVBA Rookie of the Year and MVP.

A. Elvin Hayes

B. Wes Unseld

C. Walt Frazier

D. Earl Monroe

46. How many times in his career did John Stockton have 20 or more assists in one game?

A. 12

B. 20

C. 32

D. 35

47. He was the point guard for the Minneapolis Lakers and St. Louis Hawks from 1949-1960, winning championships for both franchises.

A. Vern Mikkelsen

B. Slater Martin

C. George Martin

D. Guy Rogers

48. This player led the league in scoring three straight seasons as a member of the Buffalo Braves.

A. Ernie DiGregorio

B. Randy Smith

C. Bill Kaufmann

D. Bob McAdoo

49. The NBA first awarded a Most Valuable Player I the 1955-1956 season. Who was the league's first MVP award winner?

A. Bob Cousy

B. Bob Pettit

C. George Mikan

D. Dolph Schayes

50. Who is the NBA career leader steals?

A. Jason Kidd

B. John Stockton

C. Slick Watts

D. Gary Payton

51. The NBA All-Rookie Team in 1970-1971 included Dave Cowens, Bob Lanier, Pete Maravich, Calvin Murphy, and Geoff Petrie. Who was the Rookie of the Year?

A. Dave Cowens

B. Pete Maravich

C. Geoff Petrie

D. Bob Lanier

52. In 1961-1962, Cincinnati's Oscar Robertson became the first player to accomplish this feat in the NBA.

A. Score more than half of his team's points in a season

B. Average a triple double (points, rebounds, assists) for a season

C. Play a game without shoes

D. Wear a headband during a game

53. In the 1972-1973 season, this player led the NBA in both scoring and assists.

A. Dave Bing

B. Rick Berry

C. Pete Maravich

D. Nate Archibald

54. True or False. Reggie Miller played his entire career with the Indiana Pacers.

55. What player holds the record for most steals in a season?

A. Alvin Robertson

B. Don Buse

C. Magic Johnson

D. Slick Watts

56. How many times did Bill Russell lead the NBA in rebounds?

A. 0

B. 2

C. 5

D. 6

57. Robert Parish played 21 seasons in the NBA for four different teams. Which of these teams did he NOT play for?

A. Golden State Warriors

B. Boston Celtics

C. Chicago Bulls

D. Miami Heat

58. The top 20 highest rebound averages in a season in NBA history are held by just three players. Which player does not hold one of the top 20 spots.

A. Wilt Chamberlain

B. Jerry Lucas

C. Bill Russell

D. Nate Thurmond

59. Who holds the record for the highest rebound average per game in one season at 27.2?

A. Jerry Lucas

B. Bill Russell

C. Nate Thurmond

D. Wilt Chamberlain

60. As a rookie in 1968-1969, he led the NBA in scoring with 28.4 points per game, yet he did not win Rookie of the Year. Name the player.

A. Art Harris

B. Gary Gregor

C. Elvin Hayes

D. Earl Monroe

61. This great rebounding center was a three-time MVP while playing for the Houston Rockets and Philadelphia 76ers.

A. Ralph Sampson

B. Darryl Dawkins

C. Moses Malone

D. George McGinnis

62. The Philadelphia 76ers drafted this player, nicknamed "The Round Mound of Rebound" in the first round of the 1984 NBA draft.

A. Andre Igoudala

B. Charles Barkley

C. Billy Cunningham

D. Dolph Schayes

63. Through the 2020-2021 season, Kawhi Leonard has played for three teams. Which team has Leonard Not played for?

A. San Antonio Spurs

B. Toronto Raptors

C. Memphis Grizzlies

D. Los Angeles Clippers

64. In 19955, Kevin Garnett became the first player to be drafted out of high school by an NBA team. Which team selected him?

A. Los Angeles Lakers

B. Portland Trailblazers

C. Minnesota Timberwolves

D. Toronto Raptors

65. One of the first African American players in the NBA, Nat Clifton went by this nickname.

A. Sweetness

B. Sweetwater

C. Sweetbread

D. Cornbread

66. Michael Jordon's highest single-season scoring average was 37.1 in 1986-1987. What player or players have single season scoring average higher than that?

A. James Harden

B. Wilt Chamberlain

C. Rick Barry

D. Both A and B

67. Can you name the NBA's all-time leader in games played?

A. Vince Carter

B. Kareem Abdul-Jabbar

C. Robert Parish

D. Dirk Nowitzki

68. The 1977 NBA draft produced these top-10 picks, all of whom became All-Stars for several years. Which player was named NBA Rookie of the Year for 1977-1978?

A. Walter Davis

B. Bernard King

C. Jack Sikma

D. Marques Johnson

69. He was known as the "Iceman" and also for his patented finger roll shot.

A. Larry Kenon

B. Billy Paultz

C. George Gervin

D. Mano Ginobili

70. The record for highest season scoring average is 50.4 points per game, held by this player.

A. Michael Jordon

B. Rick Berry

C. Wilt Chamberlain

D. Kevin Durant

71. In 2017, this Phoenix Suns player scored 70 points in a losing effort against the Boston Celtics, becoming the youngest player to score that many points in NBA history.

A. Devin Booker

B. Eric Bledsoe

C. Goran Dragic

D. T.J. Warren

72. Willis Reed played his entire career with what team?

A. New Jersey Nets

B. New York Knicks

C. Cincinnati Royals

D. Philadelphia 76ers

73. This player was known as "The Mailman" because he always delivered.

A. Mark Eaton

B. Rudy Gobert

C. Adrian Dantley

D. Karl Malone

74. Who holds the single season record for most blocks?

A. Dikembe Mutombo

B. Artis Gilmore

C. Mark Eaton

D. Manute Bol

75. Who led the league in blocked shots in the first season it was recorded as an official NBA statistic, 1973-1974?

A. Elmore Smith

B. Nate Thurmond

C. Kareem Abdul Jabbar

D. Elvin Hayes

76. Leonard Robinson led the NBA in rebounding during the 1977-1978 season while playing for the New Orleans Jazz. What was his nickname?

A. Truck

B. Bulldozer

C. The Big Dipper

D. Dr. Dunkenstein

77. He was the 2018-2019 NBA Rookie of the Year.

A. Deandre Ayton

B. Luka Doncic

C. Tre Young

D. Marvin Bagley III

78. True of False. Wilt Chamberlain averaged more than 48 minutes played per game during the 1961-1962 season

79. This power forward was Rookie of the Year and a three-time All-Star in his brief three-year career with the Rochester/Cincinnati Royals. His career ended tragically in 1958.

A. Maurice Stokes

B. Jack Twyman

C. Connie Dierking

D. Clyde Lovellette

80. This player was known as "The Microwave" because he would heat up in a hurry when he came off the bench.

A. Vinny Johnson

B. Fed Brown

C. Richard Hamilton

D. Joe Dumars

81. Through the 2020-2021 season, this player holds the single season record for highest 3-point shooting percentage at .536.

A. Steve Kerr

B. Reggie Miller

C. Craig Hodges

D. Kyle Korver

82. This high-flying forward was known as "The Human Highlight Film."

A. Danny Manning

B. Joe Caldwell

C. Dominique Wilkens

D. Jamal Wilkes

83. How many seasons did Bob Cousy lead the NBA in assists?

A. 5

B. 8

C. 9

D. 10

84. True or False. Kevin McHale played for the Boston Celtics and the Minnesota Timberwolves during his playing career.

85. This Philadelphia 76er was named the league MVP for the 2000-2001 season.

A. Allen Iverson

B. Julius Erving

C. Moses Malone

D. Charles Barkley

86. During his 19-year playing career, Paul Pierce appeared in how many All-Star games?

A. 5

B. 10

C. 11

D. 14

87. In 1977-1978, the All-Rookie team was comprised of Bernard King, Marques Johnson, Walter Davis, Jack Sikma, and Norm Nixon. Which player was a rookie with the Milwaukee Bucks that season?

A. Jack Sikma

B. Walter Davis

C. Bernard King

D. Marques Johnson

88. This player has the highest career scoring average for the Toronto Raptors.

A. Vince Carter

B. Chris Bosh

C. Kyle Lowrey

D. Fred Van Fleet

89. This player starred in the NBA and ABA and was known as the "Kangaroo Kid."

A. Bill Melchionni

B. Chet Walker

C. Billy Cunningham

D. Archie Clark

90. He led the league in scoring three straight seasons, from 2017-2020 while playing for the Houston Rockets.

A. James Harden

B. Clyde Drexler

C. Chis Paul

D. Russell Westbrook

91. Through the 2020-2021 season, this player is the all-time NBA leader in points scored.

A. Karl Malone

B. Dirk Nowitzki

C. Kareem Abdul-Jabber

D. Michael Jordon

92. Who is the record holder for most rebounds in one game with 55?

A. Nate Thurmond

B. Bill Russell

C. Wilt Chamberlain

D. George Mikan

93. Who holds the single game record for blocks in one game with 15?

A. Manute Bol

B. Shaquille O'Neal

C. Mark Eaton

D. A and B

94. This player is the all-time New Jersey Nets franchise leader in assists and steals.

A. Kenny Anderson

B. Jason Kidd

C. Bill Melchionni

D. Michael Ray Richardson

95. Through the 2020-2021 season, this player has averaged a triple-double in four separate seasons.

A. Russell Westbrook

B. Kobe Bryant

C. Magic Johnson

D. Oscar Robertson

96. He starred at the University of Utah and was the 1987 NBA All-Star game MVP in front of his hometown Seattle fans.

A. Gus Williams

B. Tom Chambers

C. Jack Sikma

D. Dennis Johnson

97. Who holds the record for most triple-doubles in a season with 42?

A. Magic Johnson

B. Wilt Chamberlain

C. Russell Westbrook

D. Oscar Robertson

98. After playing collegiately at Navy, this player was known as "The Admiral" during his 14-year NBA career.

A. Armon Gilliam

B. David Robinson

C. Ed McCauley

D. Tony Parker

99. Walt Bellamy has the unique distinction of playing more games in a single season than any other NBA player. This occurred during the 1968-1969 season. How many games did he play in?

A. 82

B. 84

C. 86

D. 88

100. True or False. Eric Money is the only player in NBA history to play and score points for both teams in the same game.

101. After an impressive college career at Temple, Bill Mlkvy played one NBA season with the Philadelphia Warriors in 1952-1953. What was his nickname?

A. The Milkman

B. B-Milk

C. The Owl without a Vowel

D. Milky Way

102. Red Klotz, the long-time player coach of the Washington Generals, the team that regularly played and lost

to the Harlem Globetrotters, had a brief NBA career. Who did he play for?

A. Chicago Stags

B. Baltimore Bullets

C. Boston Celtics

D. New York Knicks

103. He averaged 24.3 points per game during his 15-year playing career, predominantly with the Utah Jazz.

A. Adrian Dantley

B. Darrell Griffith

C. Jeff Honracek

D. Rickey Green

104. This player was known to break backboards on his slam dunks.

A. Karl Malone

B. Darryl Dawkins

C. Caldwell Jones

D. Moses Malone

105. He was the NBA MVP in the 1992-1993 season following his trade to the Phoenix Suns.

A. Kevin Johnson

B. Tom Chambers

C. Charles Barkley

D. Amare Stoudemire

Answers

1. Kobe Bryant poured in 81 points for the Lakers against the Toronto Raptors in 2006.

2. George Mikan of the Minneapolis Lakers was the first dominant player in the NBA, leading the league in scoring in its first six seasons.

3. Tim Duncan of the San Antonio Spurs was known as "The Big Fundamental" for his not flashy, but fundamentally sound skills.

4. True. Through the 2020-2021 season John Stockton is the all-time NBA assist leader with 15,806.

5. Michael Jordon led the NBA in scoring ten times during his career.

6. The Milwaukee Bucks selected Antetokounmpo with the 15th pick in the 2013 NBA draft.

7. Bob Pettit played his entire career with the Hawks, first in Milwaukee and then in St. Louis.

8. Isiah Thomas played in 12 NBA All-Star games.

9. Stephen Curry and Klay Thompson formed the backcourt duo for the Golden State Warriors that became known as the "Splash Brothers."

10. Wilt Chamberlain scored 100 points in Hershey, PA, against the New York Knicks in front of a crowd of a little more than 4,000 fans.

11. Chamberlain shot 28-42 from the free throw line during his 100-point game.

12. Julius Erving was given the moniker "Dr. J."

13. Kevin Durant played for the Seattle Supersonics in his rookie season, before the franchise relocated to Oklahoma city for the following season.

14. Bill Bradley of the New York Knicks was nicknamed "Dollar Bill" for his inexpensive clothing attire.

15. True. Mark Price was a career .906 free throw shooter.

16. At only 5'3," Tyrone "Muggsy" Bogues is the shortest player ever to play in the NBA.

17. Although never charged or convicted with any point-shaving crimes during his college days, Connie Hawkins was banned from playing in the NBA by the league. After successfully suing the league, he joined the Phoenix Suns for the 1969-1970 as a 27-year-old rookie.

18. The Los Angeles Lakers drafted James Worthy with the 1982 draft pick they received via trade with Cleveland.

19. Magic Johnson was named the NBA MVP three times.

20. Dikembe Mutombo led the league in blocked shots for three straight seasons while playing for the Nuggets.

21. Kareem Abdul-Jabber won the league MVP six times, three while with the Bucks and three as a member of the Lakers.

22. Elvin Hayes was known as the "Big E" during his playing days.

23. Lebron James has averaged at least 25 points, five rebounds, and five assists in 15 different seasons through the 2020-2021 season.

24. Dwayne Wade is the Miami Heat all-time leader in assists and steals.

25. Jerry West gained the nickname "Mr. Clutch" for making late game big shots.

26. Darryl Dawkins committed an NBA record 386 fouls during the 1983-1984 season while playing for the New Jersey Nets.

27. Walt Frazier of the New York Knicks got the nickname "Clyde" for his stylish attire, reminiscent of the Bonnie and Clyde era.

28. Paul Silas never played for the San Diego Clippers.

29. Scott Skiles was credited with 30 assists in a game while playing for the Orlando Magic.

30. Patrick Ewing averaged over 20 points per game in 13 of his 15 seasons with the Knicks.

31. Although Bill Walton was the 1977-1978 MVP, he struggled with foot injuries that resulted in him missing 598 games out of a possible 1066 games, including four full seasons, due to injury during his career.

32. Steve Nash won back-to-back MVP awards while leading the Phoenix Suns in 2004-2005 and 2005-2006.

33. Larry Bird was named MVP three times.

34. Cincinnati's Adrian Smith scored 24 points in front of his home crowd as an All-Star reserve, earning game MVP honors while leading the East to a 137-94 win over the West in 1966.

35. K.C. Jones teamed with Bill Russell at the University of San Francisco as well as the Boston Celtics.

36. He was Earl "The Pearl" Monroe while playing for the Baltimore Bullets and New York Knicks.

37. On October 31, 1950, Earl Lloyd became the first African American player in the NBA when he took the floor for the Washington Capitals, scoring six points in his debut. Chuck Cooper and Nat "Sweetwater" Clifton made their debuts shortly thereafter.

38. After starring at LSU, Pete Maravich played for the Hawks and Jazz before finishing up with the Celtics.

39. False. Phil Jackson won two NBA championships as a reserve forward for the Knicks in 1969-1970 and 1973-1974.

40. Seattle's Gary Payton was known as "The Glove" for his defensive prowess.

41. Elgin Baylor was drafted by the Minneapolis Laker and moved with the team to Los Angeles, staying with the franchise for his entire playing career.

42. Dirk Nowitzki, who played his entire career with the Dalla Mavericks, is widely regarded as the best European-born player ever to play in the NBA.

43. The NBA logo features a silhouette of Lakers legend Jerry West.

44. Hakeem Olajuwon was known as "The Dream."

45. As a rookie in 1968-1969, under-sized center Wes Unseld turned the fortunes of the Baltimore Bullets around and won the NBA Rookie of the Year award and MVP.

46. Utah's John Stockton had 20 or more assists in a game on 32 different occasions.

47. Slater Martin starred at point guard for the championship Minneapolis Laker teams of the early 1950s as well as winning one title with the St. Louis Hawks in 1957-1958.

48. Bob McAdoo led the NBA in scoring three straight seasons, from 1973-1976 as a member of the Buffalo Braves.

49. Bob Pettit won the first NBA MVP award while playing for the St. Louis Hawks in 1955-1956.

50. John Stockton is the all-time leader in career steals with 3,265.

51. Geoff Petrie and Dave Cowens tied for Rookie of the Year honors.

52. Oscar Robertson averaged a triple-double for the season in 1961-1962, averaging 30.8 points, 12.5 rebounds, and 11.4 assists per game.

53. Nate Archibald, playing for the Kansas City-Omaha Kings, averaged 34.0 points and 11.4 assists per game, leading the NBA in both categories.

54. Reggie Miller starred for the Indiana Pacers, his only team, from 1987-2005.

55. Alvin Robertson had an NBA record 301 steals in the 1985-1986 season for the Spurs.

56. Bill Russell led the NBA in rebounding on five different occasions.

57. Robert Parrish never played for the Miami Heat during his playing career.

58. Wilt Chamberlain, Bill Russell, and Nate Thurmond hold all of the top 20 rebounding games. Jerry Lucas does not.

59. Wilt Chamberlain averaged 27.2 rebounds per game during the 1960-1960 season.

60. Elvin Hayes of the San Diego Rockets led the league in scoring as a rookie but lost the Rookie of the Year award to Baltimore's Wes Unseld.

61. Moses Malone was a three-time MVP, twice with the rockets and once with the 76ers.

62. The 76ers drafted Charles Barkley, known as "The Round Mound of Rebound" during his college days at Auburn, in the 1984 draft.

63. Kawhi Leonard has not played for the Memphis Grizzlies.

64. The Minnesota Timberwolves drafted Kevin Garnett in the first round of the 1995 draft.

65. Nat Clifton was known as "Sweetwater."

66. Only Wilt Chamberlain, on four separate occasions, had a single season scoring average greater than Michael Jordon.

67. Robert Parrish played in 1611 NBA games, most in history.

68. Walter Davis of the Phoenix Suns was the 1977-1978 Rookie of the Year.

69. George Gervin of the San Antonio Spurs was known as the "Iceman."

70. Wilt Chamberlain, then a member of the Philadelphia Warriors, averaged 50.4 points per game during the 1961-1962 season.

71. The Phoenix Suns Devin Booker scored 70 points in a losing effort against the Boston Celtics.

72. True. Willis Reed played his entire career, from 1964-1973, with the New York Knicks.

73. Utah's Karl Malone earned the nickname "The Mailman."

74. Utah Jazz center Mark Eaton holds the single season record for blocked shots with 456 in 1984-1985.

75. Elmore Smith, then of the Los Angeles Lakers, led the NBA in blocks in 1973-1974, with 396.

76. The NBA's leading rebounder for the 1977-1978 season was known as Leonard "Truck" Robinson.

77. The 2018-2019 Rookie of the Year was Luka Doncic of the Dallas Mavericks.

78. For the 1961-1962 season, Wilt Chamberlain actually averaged more than 48 minutes per game at 48.5 minutes per game.

79. Maurice Stokes was having a great early career with the Rochester/Cincinnati Royals before hitting his head on the floor during a game. A few days later he suffered post-traumatic encephalopathy and became paralyzed for the remainder of his life.

80. Vinnie Johnson earned the nickname "The Microwave" while playing for the Detroit Pistons.

81. Kyle Korver shot .536 from the 3-point line while playing for the Utah Jazz in 2009-2010.

82. Dominique Wilkins, who spent most of his career with the Atlanta Hawks, was known as "The Human Highlight Film."

83. Bob Cousy led the NBA in assists for eight seasons.

84. False. Kevin McHale played his entire career with the Boston Celtics.

85. Allen Iverson, known as "The Answer," was the MVP for the 2000-2001 season while a member of the Philadelphia 76ers.

86. Paul Pierce appeared in 10 All-Star games.

87. Marques Johnson was a rookie with the Milwaukee Bucks in the 1977-1978 season.

88. Vince Carter averaged 23.4 points per game while with the Toronto Raptors, the highest career scoring average for any Raptors player.

89. Billy Cunningham was known as the "Kangaroo Kid."

90. Houston's James Harden led the NBA in scoring from 2017-2020.

91. Kareem Abdul-Jabbar is the NBA's all-time leading scorer with 38,387 points over his career.

92. Wilt Chamberlain once grabbed 55 rebounds in a game against Bill Russell's Celtics in 1960.

93. Shaquille O'Neal and Manute Bol both had 15 blocks in one game. Bol did it twice.

94. Jason Kidd is the all-time Nets franchise leader in steals and assists.

95. Russell Westbrook averaged a triple-double for the 2016-2017, 2017-2018, 2018-2019, and 2020-2021 seasons.

96. Tom Chambers was the All-Star MVP in 1987 as a member of the Supersonics.

97. Russell Westbrook had 42 triple-doubles during the 2016-2017 season.

98. David Robinson of the San Antonio Spurs was knowns as "The Admiral."

99. Walt Bellamy played in 88 games during the 1968-1969 season, a result of being traded from the Knicks to the Pistons mid-season. The Piston had played fewer games than the Knicks at the time of the trade.

100. True. In 1978, The Nets lost a game to the 76ers in double overtime. However, the Nets officially protested technical fouls that had been handed out by one of the officials. The league upheld the protest and ordered the game to be replayed from the time of technical fouls. It was much later in the season when both teams could meet to replay the remaining portion of the game. In the interim, the two teams had made a trade and several players switched teams. Most of these players appeared in the replay of the game, but Eric Money was the only one of those players to score in the replay, thereby becoming the first and only player ever to play AND score for both teams in the same game.

101. Bill Mlkvy was known as "The Owl Without A Vowel."

102. Red Klotz played for the NBA champion Baltimore Bullets in 1947-1948, averaging 1.4 points per game.

103. Adrian Dantley played for seven different teams over his 15-year career, playing in six All-Star games.

104. While not the first to do it, Darryl Dawkins broke more than his share of backboards with his powerful slam dunks during his 13-year NBA career.

105. Charles Barkley was named MVP after leading the Phoenix Suns to a league-best 62-20 record in the 1992-1993 season. He average 25.6 points per game and 12.2 rebounds per game.

Coaches

In today's NBA teams have head coaches, assistant coaches, player development coaches, strength and conditioning coaches, the list goes on. When the NBA began and for years thereafter, teams had one coach. Often, that coach was also a player, as team owners did not want to pay a salary for someone to just coach.

Basketball coaching has evolved and become much more sophisticated through the years. Yet, much like great players, great coaches could coach in any era.

1. Before becoming head coach of the Chicago Bulls, Phil Jackson was the head coach of which team?

A. Detroit Pistons

B. Albany Patroons

C. Fort Wayne Mad Ants

D. New York Knicks

2. Red Auerbach became head coach of the Boston Celtics in the 1950-1951 season. What team did he coach the prior season?

A. Tri-Cities Blackhawks

B. Anderson Packers

C. St. Louis Bombers

D. Sheboygan Redskins

3. Only one of these former Boston players was ever head coach of the Celtics.

A. Frank Ramsey

B. Larry Bird

C. Danny Ainge

D. Tommy Heinsohn

4. Name the head coach of the 1947-1948 Baltimore Bullets.

A. Buddy Jeanette

B. Red Klotz

C. Red Auerbach

D. Dolph Schayes

5. He became the youngest coach in NBA history when he was named player-coach of the Detroit Pistons in 1964.

A. Terry Dischinger

B. Dave DeBusschere

C. Don Kojis

D. Donnis Butcher

6. Former Laker great Elgin Baylor coached this team from 1976-1979.

 A. Los Angeles Lakers

 B. San Diego Clippers

 C. New Orleans Jazz

 D. Buffalo Braves

7. Johnny "Red" Kerr was coach of this expansion team in 1966-1967

 A. Seattle Supersonics

 B. Chicago Bulls

 C. Phoenix Suns

 D. Milwaukee Bucks

8. In 1966, he replaced Red Auerbach as head coach of the Boston Celtics, becoming the first African American head coach in major professional sports.

A. Sam Jones

B. K.C. Jones

C. Bill Russell

D. John Thompson

9. This former Philadelphia 76ers player later coached the team from 1977-1985.

A. Chet Walker

B. Billy Cunningham

C. Matt Goukas

D. Wilt Chamberlain

10. Through the 2020-2021 season, this coach had the most wins of any head coach in NBA history.

A. Phil Jackson

B. Red Auerbach

C. Don Nelson

D. Jerry Sloan

11. Alex Hannum did NOT coach one of these teams.

A. St. Louis Hawks

B. San Diego Rockets

C. Philadelphia 76ers

D. Phoenix Suns

12. How many NBA teams did Larry Brown lead during his head coaching career?

A. 4

B. 5

C. 7

D. 9

13. How many NBA championships did Phil Jackson win as coach of the Chicago Bulls?

    A. 2

    B. 4

    C. 6

    D. 8

14. Lenny Wilkens first stint as a player-coach was with this team.

    A. Seattle Supersonics

    B. Cleveland Cavaliers

    C. St. Louis Hawks

    D. Portland Trailblazers

15. How many teams did Dick Motta coach in the NBA?

    A. 2

B. 3

C. 5

D. 6

16. Who was the first coach of the expansion Chicago Packers in 1961-1962?

A. Vern Mikkelsen

B. Jim Pollard

C. Dick Motta

D. Al Bianchi

17. The 1972-1973 Philadelphia 76ers finished with an NBA worst 9-73 record. Their first-year head coach, Roy Ruben, was fired after 51 games. What was the team's record at the time he was fired?

A. 2-49

B. 4-47

C. 8-43

D. 9-42

18.   John Kundla the highly successful coach of the Minneapolis Lakers in the early years of the NBA. In 11 seasons as coach of the Lakers, how many times did the team finish below second in their division?

A. 0

B. 1

C. 3

D. 4

19. Joe Lapchick, one of the stars of the Original Celtics in the 1920s and 1930s, coached this team from 1947-1956.

A. Philadelphia Warriors

B. Boston Celtics

C. New York Knicks

D. St. Louis Hawks

20. George Karl coached 27 year in the NBA for six different teams. Which team gave him his first head coaching opportunity?

A. Seattle Supersonics

B. Sacramento Kings

C. Cleveland Cavaliers

D. Denver Nuggets

21. The NBA first gave out the Coach of the Year award following the 1962-1963 season. Who was the first recipient?

A. Red Auerbach

B. Alex Hannum

C. Harry Gallatin

D. Paul Seymore

22. This former Boston Celtic coached the Minnesota Timberwolves and the Houston Rockets.

    A. Kevin McHale

    B. Kevin Garnett

    C. Danny Ainge

    D. K.C. Jones

23. Midway through the 1980-1981 season, Doug Moe replaced Donnie Walsh as head coach of this team. He remained head coach for the next nine seasons.

    A. San Antonio Spurs

    B. Indiana Pacers

    C. Denver Nuggets

    D. New Jersey Nets

24. Name the head coach of the "Showtime" Los Angeles Lakers in the 1980s.

A. Paul Westhead

B. Bill Bertka

C. Pat Riley

D. Phil Jackson

25. Who was the first head coach of the expansion Orlando Magic in 1989-1990?

A. Matt Goukas

B. Richie Adubato

C. Brian Hill

D. Penny Hardaway

26. Steve Kerr won an NBA championship in his first year as coach of the Golden State Warriors in 2014-2015. Who did he replace as head coach?

A. Don Nelson

B. Mark Jackson

C. Al Attles

D. Bernie Bickerstaff

27. After a seven-year playing career as a backup guard from1968-1975, he was head coach of five different NBA teams, including Portland, Sacramento, and Golden State.

A. Rick Adleman

B. Pat Riley

C. Calvin Murphy

D. John Wetzel

28. He is the longest tenured head coach of the Miami Heat.

A. Pat Riley

B. Stan Van Gundy

C. Eric Spoelstra

D. Kevin Loughery

29. Nick Nurse won the NBA championship in his first year as head coach of the Toronto Raptors in 2018-2019. The previous five seasons had been as assistant coach with the team. Prior to that, what team was he previously the head coach for?

A. Fort Wayne Mad Ants

B. Iowa Barnstormers

C. Rio Grande Vipers

D. Los Angeles Clippers

30. Who was the head coach of the San Antonio Spurs when they joined the NBA in 1976-1977?

A. Gregg Popovich

B. Doug Moe

C. Don Nelson

D. George Karl

31. Name the coach of the Detroit Pistons team, known as the "Bad Boys," from 1983-1992.

A. Scotty Robertson

B. Chuck Daly

C. Stan Van Gundy

D. Dick Vitale

32. Pat Riley was head coach of all but one of these teams. Which team did he not coach?

A. New York Knicks

B. Los Angeles Lakers

C. Phoenix Suns

D. Miami Heat

33. Who was the first coach of the expansion Seattle Supersonics in 1967-1968?

A. Al Bianchi

B. Lenny Wilkens

C. Bob Hoskins

D. Bill Russell

34. He is the only person to be head coach of both Florida franchises, Miami and Orlando.

A. Stan Van Gundy

B. Jeff Van Gundy

C. Doc Rivers

D. Ron Rothstein

35. How many championships did Red Auerbach win as head coach of the Boston Celtics?

A. 5

B. 7

C. 9

D. 10

36. He had three stints as head coach of the Phoenix Suns in 1970-1972, 1988-1992, and 1995-1996.

    A. Cotton Fitzsimmons

    B. John Wetzel

    C. John MacLeod

    D. Paul Westphal

37. Who was the first coach of the expansion New Orleans Jazz in 1974-1975?

    A. Scotty Robertson

    B. Elgin Baylor

    C. Butch Van Breda Kolff

    D. Frank Layden

38. True or False. Pat Riley never won NBA Coach of the Year.

39. Who was the coach of the New York Nets when they joined the NBA in 1976-1977?

    A. Kevin Loughery

    B. Larry Brown

    C. Don Wohl

    D. Lou Carnesecca

40. True or False. Red Auerbach never had a losing season as head coach of the Boston Celtics.

41. How many times has Gregg Popovich been named NBA Coach of the Year?

    A. 0

B. 1

C. 2

D. 3

42. True or False. Prior to taking over as coach of the San Antonio Spurs in 1996-1997 Gregg Popovich had never been a head coach in the NBA.

43. After coaching Jerry West at West Virginia, he went on to coach him again with the Los Angeles Lakers from 1960-1967.

A. Butch Van Breda Kolff

B. Fred Schaus

C. Jack McCloskey

D. John Kundla

44. Who was the first coach of the expansion Portland Trailblazers in 1970-1971?

A. Jack McCloskey

B. Roland Todd

C. Jack Ramsey

D. Kevin Loughery

45. He is the longest tenured coach in the history of the Phoenix Suns, coaching them from 1973-1987.

A. Johnny "Red" Kerr

B. John MacLeod

C. Mike D'Antoni

D. Cotton Fitzsimmons

46. This person had two stints as head coach of the Orlando Magic, 1993-1997 and 2005-2007.

A. Brian Hill

B. Stan van Gundy

C. Doc Rivers

D. Lionel Hollins

47. Butch Van Breda Kolff coached all but one of these teams.

A. Phoenix Suns

B. New Orleans Jazz

C. Memphis Grizzlies

D. Los Angeles Lakers

48. He was the head coach of the Philadelphia Warriors for the team's first nine seasons in the NBA.

A. Eddie Gottlieb

B. Al Cervi

C. Neil Johnston

D. Frank McGuire

49. How many times was Don Nelson named NBA Coach of the Year?

   A. 0

   B. 1

   C. 2

   D. 3

50. Who was the first coach of the 1967-1968 expansion San Diego Rockets?

   A. Jack Ramsey

   B. Pat Riley

   C. Jack McMahon

   D. Alex Hannum

51. Who was the first African American coach to win the Coach of the Year award?

    A. Don Chaney

    B. Ray Scott

    C. K.C. Jones

    D. Bill Russell

52. Doc Rivers has coached all but one of these teams.

    A. Orlando Magic

    B. Los Angeles Clippers

    C. New York Knicks

    D. Boston Celtics

53. Through the 2020-2021 season, which coach has the all-time highest winning percentage?

    A. Greg Popovich

B. Steve Kerr

C. Dick Motta

D. Phil Jackson

54. He was fired as coach of the Phoenix Suns after just seven games into the 1972-1973 season.

A. Cotton Fitzsimmons

B. Butch Van Breda Kolff

C. Johnny "Red" Kerr

D. John MacLeod

55. Since 1989-1990, the Utah Jazz have had only three head coaches. One of these men did not coach the Jazz during that span.

A. Tyrone Corbin

B. Jerry Sloan

C. Tom Nissalke

D. Quin Snyder

56. Although he only had a six-year NBA career as a bench player from 1984-1990, this coach has had a lengthy career as an NBA head coach, including stints with Detroit, Dallas, and Indiana.

    A. Rick Carlisle

    B. Bobby "Slick" Leonard

    C. Dick Motta

    D. Pat Riley

57. True or False. Bill Russell was named NBA Coach of the Year in 1969.

58. He is the longest tenured coach in the history of the Warriors franchise.

    A. Alex Hannum

B. Don Nelson

C. Al Attles

D. Steve Kerr

59. Who was the coach of the expansion Buffalo Braves in 1970-1971?

A. Johnny "Red" Kerr

B. Jack Seymore

C. Jack Ramsey

D. Dolph Schayes

60. Who was the first head coach of the Toronto Raptors in 1995-1996?

A. Brendan Malone

B. Karl Malone

C. Darrell Walker

D. Chet Walker

61. Who was the head coach of the Indiana Pacers when they joined the NBA in 1976-1977?

    A. Jack Ramsey

    B. George Irvine

    C. Bob "Slick" Leonard

    D. Mel Daniels

62. K.C. Jones was head coach for all but one of these teams.

    A. Washington Bullets

    B. Golden State Warriors

    C. Boston Celtics

    D. Seattle Supersonics

63. Prior to coaching the New York Knicks, Red Holzman was a player in the NBA for six seasons. Which team did he play five of those seasons for?

A. Cincinnati Royals

B. Rochester Royals

C. Fort Wayne Pistons

D. Philadelphia Warriors

64. Jerry Sloan coached this team from 1988-2011, compiling a .623 winning percentage during that time.

A. New Orleans Jazz

B. Utah Jazz

C. Chicago Bulls

D. Detroit Pistons

65. This former Boston Celtic great went on to coach the Indiana Pacers.

A. Danny Ainge

B. Bill Sharman

C. Larry Bird

D. Nate Archibald

66. Who was the first coach of the expansion Milwaukee Bucks in 1969-1970?

A. Dick Cunningham

B. Tom Nissalke

C. Larry Costello

D. Greg Smith

67. After a 12-year playing career with Seattle from 1986-1988, he has gone on to be head coach for several teams, including Seattle, Portland, Atlanta, and Indiana.

A. Gary Payton

B. Lenny Wilkens

C. Nate McMillen

D. Paul Silas

68. Who succeeded Red Holzman as coach of the New York Knicks in 1977?

A. Walt Frazier

B. Bill Bradley

C. Willis Reed

D. Phil Jackson

69. This player-coach was at the helm of the St. Louis/Atlanta Hawks from 1964-1970. He coached the team for two more seasons following his retirement as a player.

A. Cliff Hagan

B. Richie Guerin

C. Lenny Wilkens

D. Bob Pettit

70. How many times has Tom Thibodeau been named Coach of the Year?

    A. 0

    B. 1

    C. 2

    D. 3

71. Who replaced Bill Russell as coach of the Boston Celtics in 1969?

    A. Bob Cousy

    B. K.C. Jones

    C. Tom Heinsohn

    D. Bill Fitch

72. How many times has Mike Budenholzer been named Coach of the Year?

    A. 0

B. 1

C. 2

D. 3

73. Johnny Kerr also coached this expansion team in 1968-1969.

A. Phoenix Suns

B. Milwaukee Bucks

C. Cleveland Cavaliers

D. Portland Trailblazers

74. Who was the first coach of the expansion Minnesota Timberwolves in 1989-1990?

A. Flip Saunders

B. Bill Musselman

C. Larry Brown

D. Hubie Brown

75. This former player from 1954-1964 also had a lengthy head coaching career, including two separate stints coaching the Bullets from 1966-1973 and 1980-1986.

A. Gene Shue

B. Jack Ramsey

C. K.C. Jones

D. Bernie Bickerstaff

76. Jack Ramsey coached all but one of these teams.

A. Buffalo Braves

B. Portland Trailblazers

C. Denver Nuggets

D. Philadelphia 76ers

77. Who was the head coach of the Denver Nuggets when they joined the NBA in 1976-1977?

    A. Paul Westhead

    B. Doug Moe

    C. Bob Bass

    D. Larry Brown

78. Who was the first coach of the expansion Miami Heat in 1988-1989?

    A. Ron Rothstein

    B. Pat Riley

    C. Kevin Loughery

    D. Alvin Gentry

79. Chuck Daly was head coach of all but one of these teams. Which team did he never coach?

    A. Detroit Pistons

B. Minnesota Timberwolves

C. New Jersey Nets

D. Orlando Magic

80. True or False. Former Boston Celtics great, Bill Sharman, later coached both the Celtics and the Los Angeles Lakers.

81. Paul Westphal was head coach of all but one of these teams.

A. Phoenix Suns

B. Sacramento Kings

C. Seattle Supersonics

D. Brooklyn Nets

82. How many NBA championships did Phil Jackson win as head coach of the Los Angeles Lakers?

A. 2

B. 3

C. 4

D. 5

83. Who was the first coach of the expansion Cleveland Cavaliers in 1970-1971?

A. Bill Fitch

B. Lenny Wilkins

C. George Karl

D. Stan Albeck

84. He was head coach of the Phoenix Suns from 2003-2008 when their offense was known as "seven seconds or less."

A. Cotton Fitzsimmons

B. Mike D'Antoni

C. Terry Porter

D. Alvin Gentry

85. Who was the first coach of the expansion Charlotte Hornets in 1988-1989?

A. Matt Goukas

B. Ed Badger

C. Rick Adelman

D. Dick Harter

86. Who holds the record for coaching the most seasons in the NBA through the 2020-2021 season?

A. Don Nelson

B. Greg Popovich

C. Kevin Loughery

D. Lenny Wilkins

87. Bill Fitch coached all but one of these teams.

A. Cleveland Cavaliers

B. Boston Celtics

C. Houston Rockets

D. Utah Jazz

88. After playing all of his 11 seasons with the Rockets, he went on to coach the team for 12 seasons.

A. Hakeem Olajuwon

B. Rudy Tomjanovich

C. Kenny Smith

D. Ralph Sampson

89. Longtime college coach Rick Pitino had two stints as an NBA head coach, with the New York Knicks (two seasons) and the Boston Celtics (3-plus seasons). How many times did

he have a winning regular season record as an NBA head coach?

A. 1

B. 2

C. 3

D. 4

90. Often, a successful college coach does not translate well to the NBA. This highly successful college coach, most notably at Kentucky, had an unsuccessful run as head coach of the New Jersey Nets from 1996-1999.

A. John Calipari

B. Bobby Knight

C. Dean Smith

D. Dick Vitale

91. How many times did Cotton Fitzsimmons win the NBA Coach of the Year award?

    A. 0

    B. 1

    C. 2

    D. 3

92. Mike D'Antoni was the 2004-2005 Coach of the Year while head coach of the Phoenix Suns. He won the award again in 2017-2018 while coaching this team.

    A. New York Knicks

    B. Los Angeles Lakers

    C. Houston Rockets

    D. Brooklyn Nets

93. Who was the first coach of the expansion Charlotte Bobcats in 2004-2005?

A. Bernie Bickerstaff

B. Gene Shue

C. Eric Spoelstra

D. Gene Littles

94. This coach had two stints as head coach of the Golden State Warriors, 1988-1995 and 2006-2010.

A. Al Attles

B. Frank McGuire

C. Rick Adleman

D. Don Nelson

95. The Toronto Raptors head coach won the Coach of the Year award 2017-2018 and 2019-2020. Name the coach or coaches who won.

A. Dwane Casey

B. Sam Mitchell

C. Nick Nurse

D. Both A & C

96. After a 5-17 start to the 1978-1979 season, he replaced Bob Hopkins as head coach of the Seattle Supersonics and led a turn around that culminated in the team playing the NBA Finals that season.

A. Paul Silas

B. Lenny Wilkens

C. George Karl

D. Dennis Johnson

97. This former coach from the University of Florida has had a successful run as a head coach in the NBA with Oklahoma City and Chicago.

A. Rick Pitino

B. Chris Mullen

C. Billy Donavan

D. Maurice Cheeks

98.   Who was the first head coach of the expansion Vancouver Grizzlies in 1995-1996?

A. Stu Jackson

B. Brian Winters

C. Alvin Gentry

D. Doc Rivers

99.   True or False. Jack Ramsey never won NBA Coach of the Year.

100.   Who replaced Don Nelson as coach of the Milwaukee Bucks in 1987?

A. Del Harris

B. Stan Albeck

C. Mike Dunleavy

D. Jack Ramsey

Answers

1. Phil Jackson coached the Albany Patroons in the Continental Basketball Association (CBA) for five years before becoming head coach of the Chicago Bulls.

2. Red Auerbach coached the Tri-Cities Blackhawks in the 1949-1950 season, leading them to a 28-29 record, his only losing season as coach in the NBA.

3. Tommy Heinsohn played for the Celtics from 1956-1965 and then coached them from 1969-1978.

4. Buddy Jeannette was a player-coach for the Baltimore Bullets from 1947-1951, leading them to a championship in the 1947-1948 season.

5. Dave DeBusschere became head coach, as well as player, of the Detroit Pistons in 1964 at the age of 24, the youngest head coach in NBA history.

6. Elgin Baylor coached the New Orleans Jazz from 1976-1979.

7. Johnny Kerr coached the expansion Chicago Bulls in 1966-1967, leading them to a playoff berth in their first season.

8. Bill Russell replaced Red Auerbach as coach of the Celtics. He was a player-coach for three seasons.

9. Billy Cunningham played for the Philadelphia 76ers from 1965-1971and 1974-1976 and coached the team from 1977-1985.

10. Through the 2020-2021 season, Don Nelson amassed 1335 coaching victories, the most in NBA history.

11. Alex Hannum was never a coach for the Phoenix Suns.

12. Larry Brown coached nine NBA teams during his career.

13. Phil Jackson led the Bulls to six titles in his tenure in Chicago.

14. Lenny Wilkens was first-time player-coach with the Seattle Supersonics from 1969-1972.

15. Dick Motta coached five different teams in the NBA, including Dallas on two separate occasions.

16. Jim Pollard was the coach of the expansion Chicago Packers in 1961-1962.

17. The Philadelphia 76ers record at the time Roy Rubin was fired as head coach was 4-47.

18. The Minneapolis Lakers never finished below second place in their division with John Kundla as head coach for a full season.

19. Joe Lapchick coached the New York Knicks from 1947-1956.

20. George Karl's first head coaching opportunity was the Cleveland Cavaliers in 1984-1985.

21. Harry Gallatin won the first NBA Coach of the Year award in 1963 after leading the St. Louis Hawks to a 48-32 regular season record.

22. Kevin McHale coached the Minnesota Timberwolves for one full season and one partial season and later coached the Houston Rockets for five seasons.

23. Doug Moe coached the Denver Nuggets from 1980-1990.

24. Pat Riley coached the Los Angeles Lakers from 1981-1990.

25. Matt Goukas was the first coach of the Orlando Magic, leading them to an 18-64 first-year record.

26. Steve Kerr replaced Mark Jackson as head coach of the Golden State Warriors.

27. Rick Adleman coached several NBA teams following the end of his playing career.

28. Through the 2020-2021 season, Eric Spoelstra has coached the Miami Heat 13 seasons, longest of any coach in team history.

29. Prior to coaching with the Toronto Raptors, Nick Nurse coached the Rio Grande Valley Vipers in the D League.

30. Doug Moe was coach of the Spurs when they first joined the NBA.

31. Chuck Daly was the coach of the Detroit Pistons when they were known as the "Bad Boys."

32. Pat Riley played for, but never coached the Phoenix Suns.

33. Al Bianchi was the first coach of the Seattle Supersonics, leading them to a 23-59 record in the 1967-1968 season.

34. Stan Van Gundy coached the Miami Heat from 2003-2006 and the Orlando Magic from 2007-2012.

35. Red Auerbach won nine NBA championships while coaching the Boston Celtics.

36. Cotton Fitzsimmons coached the Phoenix Suns from 1970-1972, from 1988-1992, and then yet again from 1995-1996.

37. Scotty Robertson was the first head coach of the New Orleans Jazz. However, he was fired after only 15 games, going 1-14 in the process.

38. False. Pat Riley has been named Coach of the Year three separate times—while coaching three separate teams.

39. Kevin Loughery was the coach of the New Jersey Nets when the team first joined the NBA.

40. True. Red Auerbach's worst record while coaching the Celtics was 36-36 in 1954-1955.

41. Greg Popovich has been named NBA Coach of the Year three times.

42. True. Greg Popovich had been an assistant coach and a team executive, but not a head coach before becoming head coach of the Spurs.

43. Fred Schaus followed Jerry West from West Virginia to Los Angeles, where he became head coach of the Lakers.

44. Roland Todd was the first coach of the Portland Trailblazers, guiding them to a 29-53 record.

45. John Macleod coached the Phoenix Suns for 14 seasons, from 1973-1987, longer than any other coach in franchise history.

46. Brian Hill coached the Orlando Magic from 1990-1997 and 2005-2007.

47. Butch van Breda Kolff never coached the Memphis Grizzlies.

48. Eddie Gottlieb was the first coach of the Philadelphia Warriors.

49. Don Nelson was NBA Coach of the Year three times, twice with the Milwaukee Bucks and once with the Colden State Warriors.

50. Jack McMahon was the first coach of the San Diego Rockets. The Rockets went 15-67 in the team's first season.

51. Ray Scott was named NBA Coach of the Year in 1974 after leading the Detroit Pistons to a 52-30 regular season record.

52. Doc Rivers never coached the New York Knicks.

53. Phil Jackson has the top winning percentage among NBA coaches with a .704 winning percentage.

54. Butch Van Breda Kolff coached only seven games for the Phoenix Suns in the 1972-1973 season before being fired.

55. Tom Nissalke coached the Jazz from 1979-1982.

56. Rick Carlisle has had a lengthy NBA coaching career, with 20 seasons and counting.

57. False. Bill Russell was not named Coach of the Year in 1969. Gene Shue, Baltimore's coach won the award that season.

58. Al Attles coached the Golden State Warriors for 14 seasons, longer than any other in franchise history.

59. Dolph Schayes was the first coach for the Buffalo Braves, guiding them to a 22-60 regular season record.

60. Brendan Malone was the first coach of the Toronto Raptors. They finished with a 21-61 regular in season record their first season.

61. Bob "Slick" Leonard was coach of the Indiana Pacers when they first joined the NBA.

62. K.C. Jones never coached the Golden State Warriors.

63. Red Holzman played for the Rochester Royals for five of his six seasons as a player.

64. Jerry Sloan was the long-time coach of the Utah Jazz.

65. Former Celtic Larry Bird coached the Indiana Pacers from 1997-2000.

66. Larry Costello was the first coach of the Milwaukee Bucks, leading them to a 27-55 first year regular season record.

67. Following his playing career, all with Seattle, Nate McMillan has had an 18-year head coaching career—and counting.

68. Willis Reed replaced Red Holzman as coach of the New York Knicks in 1977.

69. Richie Guerin was player-coach of the Hawks and coached the team for two more seasons once he retired as a player.

70. Tom Thibodeau has been named Coach of the Year on two occasions, once while coaching the Chicago Bulls and once while leading the New York Knicks.

71. Tom Heinsohn replaced Bill Russell as coach of the Boston Celtics for the 1969-1970 season.

72. Mike Budenholzer has won the Coach of the Year award twice; once with the Atlanta Hawks and once with the Milwaukee Bucks.

73. Johnny Kerr coached the Phoenix Suns for their first season, finishing with a 16-66 regular season record.

74. Bill Musselman was the first coach of the Minnesota Timberwolves, leading them to 22-60 first year regular season record.

75. Gene Shue was a two-time coach of the Baltimore/Washington Bullets.

76. Jack Ramsey never coached the Denver Nuggets.

77. Larry Brown was the coach of the Denver Nuggets when the franchise joined the NBA.

78. Ron Rothstein was the first coach of the Miami Heat, guiding the expansion team to a 15-67 regular season record.

79. Chuck Daly never coached the Minnesota Timberwolves.

80. False. Bill Sharman coached the Los Angeles Lakers, but never coached the Boston Celtics.

81. Paul Westphal was an assistant coach for the Brooklyn Nets but was never their head coach.

82. Phil Jackson won five NBA championships as coach of the Los Angeles Lakers.

83. Bill Fitch was the first coach of the Cleveland Cavaliers, leading the team to a 15-67 first year regular season record.

84. Mike D'Antoni coached the Phoenix Suns from 2003-2008.

85. Dick Harter was the first coach of the Charlotte Hornets in the 1988-1989 season, finishing with a 20-62 regular season record.

86. Lenny Wilkens has coached the most seasons in the NBA, coaching for 32 seasons.

87. Bill Fitch never coached the Utah Jazz.

88. Rudy Tomjanovich coached the Houston Rockets after a lengthy playing career with the team.

89. Rick Pitino had one winning season as head coach in the NBA.

90. John Calipari had a .391 winning percentage in two-plus seasons as head coach of the New Jersey Nets.

91. Cotton Fitzsimmons was named Coach of the Year twice, once with the Kansas City Kings and once with the Phoenix Suns.

92. Mike D'Antoni also won Coach of the Year while coaching the Houston Rockets.

93. Bernie Bickerstaff was the first coach of the Charlotte Bobcats as they went 18-64 in their first season.

94. Don Nelson coached the Golden State Warriors on two separate occasions.

95. Dwane Casey and Nick Nurse both won NBA Coach of the Year while guiding the Toronto Raptors.

96. Lenny Wilkens took over for Bob Hopkins and led the Seattle Supersonics to the NBA Finals after a 5-17 start to the season.

97. Billy Donovan has been one of the few college coaches who has been successful as an NBA head coach.

98. Brian Winters was the first head coach of the Vancouver Grizzlies, leading the team to a 15-67 regular season record.

99. True. Jack Ramsey was never named Coach of the Year.

100. Del Harris replaced Don Nelson as coach of the Milwaukee Bucks.

The ABA

The American Basketball Association had a short, but colorful history. Beginning in 1967, the league was intent on challenging the established NBA by offering fans a more exciting, wide open brand of basketball. Yet, the league had many moving franchises, low attendance, and some owners with very little money.

There were many flamboyant players and owners and plenty of big afros. It turns out, the ABA also had some great talent. Several big-name NBA players jumped to the ABA, once they cleared legal hurdles. Some of them eventually jumped back to the NBA. The end of the ABA arrived when it finally merged with the NBA in 1976. Four ABA franchises were absorbed into the NBA with the rest of the players dispersed by a draft throughout the league.

1. Who was the first commissioner of the ABA?

   A. David Stern

   B. George Mikan

   C. Abe Saperstein

   D. Mike Storen

2. To make the ABA brand of basketball more exciting, the league introduced this innovation.

   A. Unlimited personal fouls

   B. No free throw shooting

   C. The 3-point shot

   D. 10 second shot clock

3. What color was the basketball used in ABA games?

   A. Brown

   B. Red, white, and blue

C. Brown and white

D. Orange and white

4. How many franchises were in the first season of the ABA in 1967-1968?

    A. 8

    B. 10

    C. 11

    D. 14

5. Who led the league in scoring in the first ABA season?

    A. Doug Moe

    B. Larry Brown

    C. Connie Hawkins

    D. Lavern Tart

6. This NBA All-Star had to sit out a season due to contractual issues with the San Francisco Warriors after jumping from the NBA to the ABA in 1968.

    A. Rick Barry

    B. Wilt Chamberlain

    C. Al Attles

    D. Nate Thurmond

7. What was the name of the Oakland franchise?

    A. Oaks

    B. Athletics

    C. Bays

    D. Pines

8. After two seasons in Oakland, the franchise moved to Washington, DC, for one season before settling in Virginia. What was the team name while in Virginia?

A. Pipers

B. Squares

C. Squires

D. Beaches

9. Who was the league MVP for the 1967-1968 season?

    A. Louie Dampier

    B. Connie Hawkins

    C. Mel Daniels

    D. Freddie Lewis

10. The Utah Stars franchise was located in what city and played under what name in the ABA's first year?

    A. Los Angeles Stars

    B. Anaheim Ducks

    C. Anaheim Amigos

D. Los Angeles Amigos

11. Who is the all-time leader in career rebounds?

   A. Mel Daniels

   B. Artis Gilmore

   C. Gerald Govan

   D. Bob Netolicky

12. The San Antonio Spurs franchise started out as this team.

   A. Dallas Mavericks

   B. Dallas Chapparals

   C. Houston Fleas

   D. New Orleans Buccaneers

13. What team did Larry Brown first coach in the ABA?

A. Denver Nuggets

B. Carolina Cougars

C. New York Nets

D. San Antonio Spurs

14. Which team won the first ABA championship in 1967-1968?

A. Minnesota Pipers

B. Oakland Oaks

C. Pittsburgh Pipers

D. New Orleans Buccaneers

15. Doug Moe and Larry Brown teamed up to form a dynamic duo that led this team into the first ABA championship series.

A. Pittsburgh Pipers

B. New Orleans Buccaneers

C. Oakland Oaks

D. Anaheim Amigos

16. Bob "Slick" Leonard coached the Indiana Pacers for all but their inaugural ABA season. Who was the first coach of the Pacers?

    A. Tom Meschery

    B. Larry Staverman

    C. Kevin Loughery

    D. Babe McCarthy

17. He is the all-time leading scorer in the ABA.

    A. Louie Dampier

    B. Dan Isscl

    C. Julius Erving

    D. Mel Daniels

18. Who was the league MVP for the 1968-1969 season?

    A. Rick Barry

    B. Steve Jones

    C. Connie Hawkins

    D. Mel Daniels

19. After one year playing with the Cincinnati Royals in the NBA, this guard had a lengthy ABA career, including three All-Star appearances, primarily with the Indiana Pacers.

    A. Freddie Lewis

    B. Doug Moe

    C. Mack Calvin

    D. Goo Kennedy

20. What team won the ABA championship in 1968-1969?

    A. Oakland Oaks

B. Kentucky Colonels

C. Indiana Pacers

D. New York Nets

21. What player has the highest single-season scoring average in the ABA?

A. Rick Barry

B. Spencer Haywood

C. Julius Erving

D. Charlie Scott

22. Bruce Hale, who was also Rick Barry's father-in-law coached this team in the first ABA season.

A. Miami Floridians

B. Virginia Squires

C. Oakland Oaks

D. Denver Nuggets

23. What was Julius Erving's career scoring average in the ABA?

    A. 27.72

    B. 28.65

    C. 31.10

    D. 33.65

24. This former NBA player and coach was the coach of the Oakland Oaks and the Denver Nuggets in the ABA.

    A. Bill Sharman

    B. Alex Hannum

    C. Al Bianchi

    D. Slater Martin

25. This forward-center starred with the Kentucky Colonels in the ABA and the Denver Nuggets in the ABA and NBA.

    A. Louie Dampier

    B. Dan Issel

    C. Bird Averitt

    D. Byron Beck

26. Another NBA All-Star left the Philadelphia 76ers in 1972 to join the Carolina Cougars.

    A. Matt Goukas

    B. Lucious Jackson

    C. Billy Cunningham

    D. Hal Greer

27. This former Celtics great coached the Los Angeles/Utah Stars for three seasons, leading them to the championship in 1970-1971.

A. Bob Cousy

B. K.C. Jones

C. Bill Sharman

D. Bailey Howell

28. What team did Doug Moe first coach in the ABA?

A. Utah Stars

B. San Antonio Spurs

C. Denver Nuggets

D. Memphis Tams

29. Who was the league MVP in the 1969-1970 season?

A. Bob Verga

B. Rick Barry

C. Spencer Haywood

D. Doug Moe

30. What was the name of the Miami ABA franchise?

A. Floridians

B. Palms

C. Flames

D. Sails

31. Who is the all-time ABA leader in 3-point shots made?

A. Roger Brown

B. Freddie Lewis

C. Louie Dampier

D. Bill Keller

32. Who is the ABA all-time leader in steals?

A. Julius Erving

B. Fatty Taylor

C. Don Buse

D. Ralph Simpson

33. Name the player with the highest single season rebounding average in the ABA?

A. Artis Gilmore

B. Spencer Haywood

C. Mel Daniels

D. Julius Keye

34. George Gervin spent most of his stellar career with the San Antonio Spurs in both the ABA and NBA. What team did he first play for?

A. Virginia Squires

B. Indiana Pacers

C. Spirits of St. Louis

D. Utah Stars

35. Who was Julius Erving's first coach when he was a rookie with the Virginia Squires?

    A. Bill Musselman

    B. Bruce Hale

    C. Alex Hannum

    D. Al Bianchi

36. This big, slow center played for the New Yok Nets and the San Antonio Spurs while in the ABA and was known as "The Whopper."

    A. Artis Gilmore

    B. Mel Daniels

    C. Billy Paultz

    D. Swen Nater

37. True or False. Artis Gilmore let the ABA in rebounds in four of his five ABA seasons?

38. Who was the league MVP for the 1970-1971 season?

   A. Mel Daniels

   B. Mack Calvin

   C. Charlie Scott

   D. Zelmo Beaty

39. The Memphis franchise was known by several names. One of these was not a team name for Memphis.

   A. Pros

   B. Tams

   C. Sounds

   D. Blues

40. After jumping to the ABA from the Atlanta Hawks, Zelmo Beaty starred for what team?

    A. Memphis Pros

    B. Spirits of St. Louis

    C. Utah Stars

    D. Denver Nuggets

41. Who was the league MVP for the 1971-1972 season?

    A. Dan Issel

    B. Rick Barry

    C. Artis Gilmore

    D. Willie Wise

42. What coach has the most career wins in ABA history?

    A. Babe McCarthy

    B. Bob Bass

C. Bob "Sick" Leonard

D. Al Bianchi

43. This team started out as the Houston Mavericks, then moved to Carolina and became the Cougars. The franchise later moved one last time to become what team?

A. Miami Floridians

B. Spirits of St. Louis

C. Baltimore Claws

D. Memphis Tams

44. Who is the all-time leader in assists?

A. Bill Melchionni

B. Mack Calvin

C. Louie Dampier

D. Freddie Lewis

45. This long-time NBA coach and later television analyst coached the Kentucky Colonels to the championship in 1974-1975.

    A. Tom Nissalke

    B. Hubie Brown

    C. Larry Brown

    D. Babe McCarthy

46. He played two seasons for the Spirts of St. Louis and was known, for good reasons, as "Bad News."

    A. Joe Caldwell

    B. Don Adams

    C. Marvin Barnes

    D. Maurice Lucas

47. True or False, the Memphis franchise was, for a time, known as the Tams and it was an acronym for Tennessee, Arkansas, and Mississippi.

48. This NBA legend was head coach of the San Diego Conquistadors for 1973-1974 season.

   A. Bill Russell

   B. Elgin Baylor

   C. Bob Cousy

   D. Wilt Chamberlain

49. Who was the league MVP for the 1972-1973 season?

   A. Julius Erving

   B. Billy Cunningham

   C. Warren Jabali

   D. Ralph Simpson

50. Ron Boone was a four-time All-Star and had a stellar ABA career playing for all but one of these teams.

    A. Utah Stars

    B. Dallas Chapparals

    C. New York Nets

    D. Spirits of St. Louis

51. This former St. Louis Hawks player was a player-coach for the Dallas Chapparals from 1967-1970.

    A. Cliff Hagan

    B. Bob Pettit

    C. Slater Martin

    D. Lenny Wilkens

52. Who was the league MVP for the 1973-1974 season?

    A. Julius Erving

B. George McGinnis

C. Artis Gilmore

D. Dan Issel

53. Which player has the highest single season assists per game average?

A. Larry Brown

B. Don Buse

C. Mack Calvin

D. Bill Melchionni

54. Which coach had the highest all-time winning percentage in the ABA?

A. LaDell Andersen

B. Vince Cazzetta

C. Larry Brown

D. Bob "Slick" Leonard

55. Which team won the ABA championship in 1973-1974?

A. New York Nets

B. Utah Stars

C. Kentucky Colonels

D. Indiana Pacers

56. Who was the league MVP for the 1974-1975 season?

A. George McGinnis

B. Swen Nater

C. Julius Erving

D. Marvin Barnes

57. Name the player with the highest single season steals per game average.

A. Brian Taylor

B. Fatty Taylor

C. Don Buse

D. Ted McClain

58. Who was the last ABA Rookie of the Year in 1975-1976?

A. Marvin Webster

B. Dan Olberding

C. David Thompson

D. Dan Roundfield

59. Who was the last ABA champion in 1975-1976?

A. Denver Nuggets

B. New York Nets

C. Utah Stars

D. Kentucky Colonels

60. Who was the last league MVP for the 1975-1976 season?

A. Julius Erving

B. Bobby Jones

C. James Silas

D. David Thompson

Answers

1. Former Minneapolis Laker great George Mikan was the first commissioner of the ABA. He served in that role from 1967 to 1969.

2. The ABA introduced the 3-point shot for its inaugural season in 1967-1968 and it was later adopted by the NBA a few years after the NBA-ABA merger. It remains a major weapon in today's game.

3. The ABA used a red, white, and blue ball. Commissioner Mikan believed it would be better to see on television.

4. There were 11 franchises when the ABA played its first season.

5. Connie Hawkins, playing for the Pittsburgh Pipers, was the league's first scoring champion, averaging 26.79 points per game.

6. After jumping to the ABA's Oakland franchise, Rick Barry was forced by the courts to sit out a year due to legal contractual issues.

7. The ABA franchise in Oakland was known as the Oaks.

8. Following the relocation of the franchise to Virginia, the team became known as the Squires.

9. Connie Hawkins was the ABA's first MVP in 1967-1968.

10. The franchise started out as the Anaheim Amigos before becoming the Los Angeles Stars and then finally moving to Utah but remained known as the Stars.

11. Mel Daniels of the Indiana Pacers is the career leader in rebounds with 9494.

12. The Spurs franchise began as the Dallas Chapparals.

13. Larry Brown's first head coaching stint was with the Carolina Cougars in 1972-1973.

14. The Connie Hawkins-led Pittsburgh Pipers defeated the New Orleans Buccaneers to win the first ever ABA championship.

15. Point guard Larry Brown and scoring forward Doug Moe led the New Orleans Buccaneers into the 1967-1968 championship series against Pittsburgh.

16. Larry Staverman coached the Indiana Pacers for the team's first season. He was fired nine game into their second season and Slick Leonard took over.

17. Louie Dampier is the all-time leading scorer in the ABA with 13,726 points.

18. Mel Daniels of the Indiana Pacers was the league MVP for the 1968-1969 season.

19. Freddie Lewis starred for the Indiana Pacers for most of his ABA career, averaging 17.0 points per game over nine total ABA seasons.

20. The Oakland Oaks defeated the Indiana Pacers to win the ABA championship in 1968-1969.

21. Charlie Scott has the highest single-season scoring average with 34.58 points per game in 1971-1972.

22. Bruce Hale coached the Oakland Oaks in the ABA's firs season, amassing a 22-56 record.

23. Julius Erving's ABA career scoring average was 28.65 points per game.

24. In addition to lengthy coaching stints in the NBA, Alex Hannum coached the Oakland Oaks and Denver Nuggets in the ABA.

25. Dan Issel played for both the Kentucky Colonels and the Denver Nuggets in the ABA and had an ABA career scoring average of 25.65 points per game.

26. Billy Cunningham played two seasons for the Carolina Cougars before jumping back to the Philadelphia 76ers.

27. Bill Sharman coached the Los Angeles/Utah Stars from 1969-1971.

28. Doug Moe's first head coaching job was with the San Antonio Spurs.

29. Spencer Haywood of the Denver Nuggets was the league MVP for the 1969-1970 season.

30. The Miami team was called the Floridians.

31. Louie Dampier is the all-time leader in career 3-point shots made with 794.

32. Fatty Taylor is the all-time leader in career steals with 803.

33. Spencer Haywood pulled down 19.49 rebounds per game in 1969-1970.

34. George Gervin first played for the Virginia Acquires.

35. Julius Erving's first coach in the ABA was Al Bianchi, who coached the Virginia Squires for six-plus seasons from 1970-1976.

36. Billy Paultz was known as "The Whopper."

37. True. Artis Gilmore led the league in rebounding for three seasons, from 1971-1974 and again in 1975-1976.

38. Mel Daniels of the Indiana Pacers was the league MVP for the 1970-1971 season.

39. The Memphis franchise was never known as the Memphis Blues.

40. Zelmo Beatty jumped from the NBA's Atlanta Hawks to play for the Utah Stars, although he did have to sit out the entire 1969-1970 season before he could join the Stars.

41. Artis Gilmore of the Kentucky Colonels was the league's MVP in 1971-1972.

42. Bob "Slick" Leonard amassed 387 ABA coaching wins, over 90 more than any other coach.

43. The franchise finally ended up in St. Louis and became known as the Spirits of St. Louis.

44. Louis Dampier is the ABA's all-time assists leader with 4,044.

45. Hubie Brown coached the Kentucky Colonels to the championship in 1974-1975.

46. Marvin "Bad News" Barnes played and caused havoc for the Spirits of St. Louis for two seasons.

47. True. The team believed it could draw fans from Tennessee, Arkansas, and Mississippi. It couldn't. It could barely draw fans from Memphis.

48. Former NBA great coached the San Diego Conquistadors for the 1973-1974 season, just one year

removed from winning an NBA championship with the Los Angeles Lakers. It was his one and only season as San Diego's coach.

49. Billy Cunningham of the Carolina Cougars was the league MVP for the 1972-1973 season.

50. Ron Boone never played for the New York Nets.

51. Former St. Louis Hawks player, Cliff Hagen coached and played for the Dallas Chapparals from 1967-1970

52. Julius Erving of the New York Nets was the league's MVP for the 1973-1974 season.

53. Bill Melchionni of the New York Kicks average 8.36 assists per game in 1971-1972.

54. Vince Cazzetta coached one season, leading the Pittsburgh Pipers to a 54-24 regular season record, a .692 winning percentage, the highest all-time for ABA coaches.

55. The New York Nets were the ABA champion for the 1973-1974 season.

56. A bit of a trick question as both Julius Erving of the New York Nets and George McGinnis of the Indiana Pacers were co-MVPs for the 1974-1975 season.

57. Don Buse averaged 4.12 steals per game in 1975-1976 while playing for the Indiana Pacers.

58. David Thompson of the Denver Nuggets was the Rookie of the Year in the 1975-1976 season.

59. The New York Nets defeated the Denver Nuggets to win the 1975-1976 ABA championship.

60. The ABA's last MVP was Julius Erving of the New York Nets.

Playoffs

The NBA playoffs, culminating with the NBA Finals are often where legends and reputations are made. Some teams had one great season, which resulted in a championship, while other franchises were perennial championship contenders. Each decade has had its dominant playoff teams and individual performances.

The first NBA playoffs in 1946-1947 consisted of six teams, the top three from each of the two divisions. That season, there were a total of 19 playoff games played to determine the league champion. Current playoff formats consist of 16 teams, the top eight from each conference. To win the NBA title today, the champion must win four playoff series.

1. Who is the NBA's all-time leading scorer in the playoffs?

    A. Michael Jordon

    B. Wilt Chamberlain

    C. Lebron James

    D. Kareem Abdul Jabbar

2. How many championships did Bill Russell win during his 13-year playing career with the Boston Celtics?

    A. 5

    B. 7

    C. 9

    D. 11

3. This player was named the NBA Finals MVP despite playing on the losing team.

    A. Patrick Ewing

B. Jerry West

C. Karl Malone

D. Wilt Chamberlain

4. How many championships did George Mikan win during his nine-year NBA career, primarily with the Minneapolis Lakers?

A. 2

B. 4

C. 5

D. 6

5. Name the player with the highest lifetime playoff scoring average.

A. Kevin Durant

B. James Harden

C. Stephen Curry

D. Michael Jordon

6. This NBA great toiled with the Cincinnati Royals for years without much playoff success. It wasn't until he was traded to the Milwaukee Bucks that he was able to win his one and only championship. Name the player.

  A. Jack Twyman

  B. Oscar Robertson

  C. Flynn Robinson

  D. Connie Dierking

7. True or False. Kareem Abdul Jabber was named NBA Finals MVP four times.

8. How many championships did Michael Jordon win with the Chicago Bulls?

  A. 3

B. 4

C. 5

D. 6

9. Through the 2020-2021 season, how many championships has the Warriors franchise won (Philadelphia/San Francisco/Golden State)?

A. 2

B. 4

C. 6

D. 7

10. This defensive standout was named the NBA Finals MVP in 1979.

A. Jack Sikma

B. Lonnie Shelton

C. Wes Unseld

D. Dennis Johnson

11. The Baltimore Bullets won the NBA championship in 1948, defeating the Philadelphia Warriors. Who was the team's player-coach?

    A. Red Klotz

    B. Gene Shue

    C. Buddy Jeanette

    D. Kleggie Hermsen

12. This player holds the record for most points scored in a playoff game with 63.

    A. Elgin Baylor

    B. Dwayne Wade

    C. Michael Jordon

    D. LeBron James

13. How many championships did Wilt Chamberlain win during his 14-year career with the Philadelphia/San Francisco Warriors, Philadelphia 76ers?

A. 0

B. 1

C. 2

D. 4

14. True or False. Kevin Durant has been named NBA Finals MVP three times.

15. How many times have the New York Knicks played in the NBA Finals?

A. 2

B. 4

C. 6

D. 8

16. Slater Martin was the point guard for the Minneapolis Lakers teams that won five championships from 1949-1954. He also won another championship with this team.

    A. Boston Celtics

    B. St. Louis Hawks

    C. Rochester Royals

    D. Philadelphia Warriors

17. How many championships did Sam Jones win as a member of the Boston Celtics?

    A. 4

    B. 5

    C. 8

    D. 10

18. This player has the highest lifetime playoff rebound average.

A. Moses Malone

B. Bill Russell

C. Wilt Chamberlain

D. Kareem Abdul Jabbar

19. How many championships did Bob Cousy win during his 13-year career with the Boston Celtics?

A. 4

B. 5

C. 6

D. 8

20. True or False. No team has ever overcome a 3-1 series deficit in the NBA Finals to win the championship.

21. The Boston Celtics won the NBA championship in 1968 and 1969 with this player-coach.

A. Bill Russell

B. K.C. Jones

C. Tom Heinsohn

D. Satch Sanders

22. He was the NBA Finals MVP when the Portland Trailblazers won their only NBA championship in 1977.

A. Maurice Lucas

B. Bill Walton

C. Dave Twardzik

D. Lionel Hollins

23. Game 5 of the 1976 NBA Finals featured the Phoenix Suns playing the Celtics in Boston. The game went into three overtimes and is considered by many to be the greatest game ever played. Name the player who made the basket to send the game into the third overtime?

A. Paul Westphal

B. John Havlicek

C. Dick Van Arsdale

D. Gar Heard

24. How many championships did Kobe Bryant win during his 20-year career with the Los Angeles Lakers?

A. 2

B. 3

C. 5

D. 7

25. Who holds the record for most total career playoff rebounds?

A. Kareem Abdul Jabber

B. Bill Russell

C. Wilt Chamberlain

D. Moses Malone

26. Through the 2020-2021 season, how many championships has the Lakers franchise won (Minneapolis and Los Angeles)?

A. 10

B. 12

C. 15

D. 17

27. Name the player who appeared in the most playoff games without winning a championship.

A. Steve Nash

B. Karl Malone

C. John Stockton

D. Gary Payton

28. Before they started a string of championships, Michael Jordon's Chicago Bulls lost to this team in the Eastern Conference Finals, who went on to become eventual NBA champions.

    A. New York Knicks

    B. Boston Celtics

    C. Detroit Pistons

    D. Cleveland Cavaliers

29. True or False. While coach of the Boston Celtics, Red Auerbach once won eight NBA championships in a row.

30. How many times have the Boston Celtics and the Minneapolis/Los Angeles Lakers met in the NBA Finals?

    A. 6

    B. 8

C. 10

D. 12

31. How many championships did Jerry West win during his 14-year career with the Los Angeles Lakers?

A. 1

B. 2

C. 4

D. 5

32. True or False. Through the 2020-2021 season, Tim Duncan has appeared in the most career playoff games in league history.

33. How many times did Bill Russell and Wilt Chamberlain meet in the NBA Finals?

A. 2

B. 4

C. 5

D. 7

34. Through the 2020-2021 season, how many championships has LeBron James won in his career with the Cleveland Cavaliers, Miami Heat, and Los Angeles Lakers?

A. 2

B. 3

C. 4

D. 6

35. This player has the highest single season playoff scoring average (minimum five games) in league history with 40.6 points per game.. He did it in 1965.

A. Jerry West

B. Elgin Baylor

C. Wilt Chamberlain

D. Oscar Robertson

36. True or False. Bill Russell was never named NBA Finals MVP.

37. Robert Horry played 16 seasons for four different teams. Known as "Big Shot Bob," he had the uncanny knack of playing for the right team at the right time as he played on seven championship teams. Of the four teams he played for, he did not win a championship with only one. Which one?

A. Houston Rockets

B. Phoenix Suns

C. Los Angeles Lakers

D. San Antonio Spurs

38. Through the 2020-2021 season, how many championships have the Boston Celtics won?

A. 12

B. 14

C. 17

D. 18

39. How many NBA Finals MVP awards has Shaquille O'Neal won?

A. 2

B. 3

C. 4

D. 5

40. This player was named NBA Finals MVP twice while playing for two different teams, the San Antonio Spurs and the Toronto Raptors.

A. Tony Parker

B. Kawhi Leonard

C. Vince Carter

D. Kyle Lowry

41. How many championships did Kareem Abdul Jabber win in his 20-year career with both the Milwaukee Bucks and Los Angeles Lakers?

    A. 3

    B. 4

    C. 6

    D. 8

42. The St. Louis Hawks played the Boston Celtics four times in the NBA Finals from 1957-1961. How many times did they beat the Celtics?

    A. 0

    B. 1

    C. 2

D. 3

43. How many times was Magic Johnson named NBA Finals MVP?

    A. 2

    B. 3

    C. 4

    D. 5

44. True or False. Charles Barkley won one NBA championship as a player.

45. This player has the highest playoff assists per game average in history.

    A. Isiah Thomas

    B. John Stockton

    C. Magic Johnson

    D. Kevin Johnson

46. True or False. Phil Jackson won 13 NBA championships as either a player or a coach.

47. There have only been two NBA Finals games that went to three overtimes. One team played in both games. Name the team.

    A. Phoenix Suns

    B. Boston Celtics

    C. Chicago Bulls

    D. St. Louis Hawks

48. Who did the Philadelphia Warriors beat in the first NBA Finals in 1947?

    A. Providence Steamrollers

    B. Pittsburgh Ironmen

    C. Chicago Stags

    D. Toronto Huskies

49. Name the player who made the game-winning 3-point shot in game 6 of the 1993 NBA Finals as the Chicago Bulls won the series, defeating the Phoenix Suns 4-2.

    A. Michael Jordon

    B. Jim Paxson

    C. Scotty Pippen

    D. Horace Grant

50. This player was the NBA Finals MVP when the Dallas Mavericks won their only NBA Championship in 2011.

    A. Jason Kidd

    B. Jason Terry

    C. Shawn Marion

    D. Dirk Nowitzki

51. From 1956-1969, the Celtics won 11 NBA championships. Only two other teams were NBA champions

during that span, the St. Louis Hawks and the Philadelphia 76ers. The same man coached both of those teams. Name the coach.

A. Al Bianchi

B. Jack Ramsey

C. Alex Hannum

D. Red Holzman

52. How many championships did Larry Bird win during his 13-year career with the Boston Celtics?

A. 1

B. 3

C. 4

D. 5

53. Through the 2020-2021 season, name the coach who has the highest playoff winning percentage.

A. Gregg Popovich

B. Steve Kerr

C. Red Holzman

D. Phil Jackson

54. Through the 2020-2021 season, LeBron James has played in 10 NBA Finals. How many times has he been named Finals MVP?

A. 0

B. 2

C. 4

D. 6

55. One of the Celtics coaches never won a championship while coaching Boston.

A. K.C. Jones

B. Bill Fitch

C. Chris Ford

D. Doc Rivers

56. This former Celtics player coached the Los Angeles Lakers to their first NBA championship in 1973.

A. Bob Cousy

B. Frank Ramsey

C. Bill Sharman

D. Bill Russell

57. How many championships did Magic Johnson win during his 13-year career with the Lakers?

A. 3

B. 4

C. 5

D. 6

58. Only one player has averaged 30 or more rebounds per game in a single post season. Name the player.

   A. Hakeem Olajuwon

   B. Moses Malone

   C. Bill Russell

   D. Wilt Chamberlain

59. True or False. Michael Jordon won NBA Finals MVP three times in a row twice.

60. How many championships has Gregg Popovich won as coach of the San Antonio Spurs?

   A. 2

   B. 3

   C. 4

   D. 6

Answers

1. LeBron James is the all-time leader in points scored in the playoffs with 7631 points through the 2020-2021 season.

2. Bill Russell led the Celtics to 11 championships in his 13 seasons.

3. Jerry West was named the 1969 Finals MVP despite his Lakers losing to the Celtics in seven games. He averaged 37.9 points per game in the series.

4. George Mikan won five championships while playing with the Minneapolis Lakers.

5. Michael Jordon has the highest career playoff scoring average at 33.5.

6. Oscar Robertson was traded by the Cincinnati Royals to the Milwaukee Bucks in 1970. He joined Kareem Abdul-Jabbar and the Bucks won the NBA championship in 1970-1971.

7. False. Kareem Abdul Jabbar was named NBA Finals MVP twice, in 1971 with the Bucks and 1985 with the Los Angeles Lakers.

8. Michael Jordon won six NBA championships with the Chicago Bulls.

9. The Warriors franchise has won six NBA titles.

10. Dennis Johnson was the NBA Finals MVP in 1979 as the Seattle Supersonics defeated the Washington Bullets.

11. Buddy Jeanette was player-coach for the 1947-1948 NBA champion Baltimore Bullets.

12. Michael Jordon scored 63 points in a playoff game in a losing effort against the Boston Celtics in 1986.

13. Wilt Chamberlain won two NBA championships in his career, one with the Philadelphia 76ers in 1967 and one with the Los Angeles Lakers in 1973.

14. False. Kevin Durant was named NBA Finals MVP with the Golden State Warriors in 2017 and 2018.

15. The New York Knicks have played in the NBA Finals eight times, winning twice.

16. Slater Martin also won a championship with the St. Louis Hawks in 1958.

17. Sam Jones won 10 championships with the Boston Celtics.

18. Bill Russell averaged 24.9 rebounds per game for his playoff career.

19. Bob Cousy won six championships during his Boston Celtics career.

20. False. The Cleveland Cavaliers overcame a 3-1 series deficit against the Golden State Warriors to become NBA champions in 2016.

21. Bill Russell was Celtics player-coach for their championships in 1968 and 1969.

22. Bill Walton was named NBA Finals MVP in 1977 as the Portland Trailblazers defeated the Philadelphia 76ers.

23. Gar Heard of the Phoenix Suns made a jump shot as time expired to send the game into a third overtime. Boston eventually won the game 128-126.

24. Kobe Bryant won five NBA championships during his career.

25. Bill Russell hauled down 4,104 total rebounds in his playoff career.

26. The Minneapolis/Los Angeles Lakers have won 17 NBA championships.

27. Karl Malone appeared in 193 playoff games without ever winning a championship.

28. The Chicago Bulls lost to the Detroit Pistons in the Eastern Conference Finals in 1988 and 1989.

29. True. Auerbach coached the Boston Celtics to eight consecutive NBA titles from 1959-1966.

30. The Celtics and Lakers have met 12 times in the NBA Finals, with the Celtics winning nine times.

31. Jerry West won one NBA title, in 1972, during his Lakers career.

32. False. LeBron James has appeared in 266 playoff games through the 2020-2021 season.

33. Bill Russell and Wilt Chamberlain met in the NBA Finals only twice, 1964 when Chamberlain was with the San Francisco Warriors and 1969 when he played for the Los Angeles Lakers.

34. Lebron James has won four NBA titles, two with Miami Heat; one with Cleveland and one with the Lakers.

35. Jerry West averaged 40.6 points per game in 11 playoff games in 1965.

36. True. The NBA did not award an MVP for the Finals until 1969, Russell's last year in the league. Jerry West won the Finals MVP that year.

37. Robert Horry won championships while playing for the Houston Rockets, Los Angeles Lakers, and San Antonio Spurs, but not with the Phoenix Suns.

38. The Boston Celtics have won 17 NBA championships.

39. Shaquille O'Neal won the NBA Finals MVP three times.

40. Kawhi Leonard was the Finals MVP in 2014 as a member of the San Antonio Spurs and again in 2019 while playing for the Toronto Raptors.

41. Kareem Abdul-Jabbar won six NBA titles, one with the Bucks and five with the Lakers.

42. The St. Louis Hawks beat the Boston Celtics only once in the NBA Finals, in 1958.

43. Magic Johnson was named Finals MVP three times.

44. False. Charles Barkley never won an NBA championship.

45. Magic Johnson averaged 12.4 assists per game in his playoff career.

46. True. Phil Jackson won six championships as coach of the Chicago Bulls, five while coaching the Los Angeles Lakers, and two as a player for the New York Knicks.

47. The Phoenix Suns lost in three overtimes in Game 5 of the 1976 Finals against the Boston Celtics and defeated the Chicago Bulls in three overtimes in Game 3 of the 1993 Finals.

48. The Philadelphia Warriors defeated the Chicago Stags to win the first NBA championship.

49. Jim Paxson drilled a 3-point shot in Game 6 of the 1993 Finals to defeat the Phoenix Suns.

50. Dirk Nowitzki of the Dallas Mavericks won the Finals MVP in 2011.

51. Alex Hannum was the coach of the 1957-1958 champion St. Louis Hawks and the 1966-1967 champion Philadelphia 76ers.

52. Larry Bird won three NBA titles during his Boston Celtics career.

53. Steve Kerr has a career playoff winning percentage of .733 through the 2020-2021 season.

54. Lebron James has been the Finals MVP four times.

55. Chris Ford did not win a championship in his five seasons as coach of the Boston Celtics.

56. Former Celtics guard Bill Sharman coached the Los Angeles Lakers for five years, leading them to the championship in 1972.

57. Magic Johnson won five championships during his Los Angeles Lakers career.

58. Wilt Chamberlain averaged 30.2 rebound per game during the 1966 playoffs.

59. True. Michael Jordan won the Finals MVP three consecutive years from 1991-1993 and again from 1996-1998.

60. Gregg Popovich has led the San Antonio Spurs to five NBA titles.

The WNBA

The WNBA began with the backing of the NBA, with some franchises being owned outright by the NBA franchises located in the same city. It coincided with and helped promote growing interest in women's basketball in general and women's professional basketball in particular.

As with any new league, there were growing pains, with some franchises folding or relocating. Of the original franchises, only four remain where they started. Yet, the league has continued to grow in popularity. Let's see what you know about the history of the WNBA.

1. What was the first season of the WNBA?

A. 1995

B. 1994

C. 1997

D. 2000

2. How many teams comprised the WNBA in the inaugural season?

A. 8

B. 10

C. 12

D. 14

3. True of False. Each team played 25 games in the first season.

4. What team was the first WNBA champion?

A. Los Angeles Sparks

B. Phoenix Mercury

C. New York Liberty

D. Houston Comets

5. Who was the first WNBA MVP?

A. Lisa Leslie

B. Cynthia Cooper

C. Jennifer Gillom

D. Rebecca Lobo

6. Through the 2021 season, who is the all-time leading scorer in WNBA history?

A. Candice Dupree

B. Sue Bird

C. Diana Taurasi

D. Tina Thompson

7. There have been four original franchises that have remained in the same city and under the same name since the inaugural season. One of these teams is NOT one of the original franchises.

    A. Los Angeles Sparks

    B. Phoenix Mercury

    C. Washington Mystics

    D. New York Liberty

8. Who is the oldest player to appear in a WNBA game?

    A. Rebecca Lobo

    B. Jennifer Gillom

    C. Nancy Lieberman

    D. Diana Taurasi

9. Former Detroit Pistons star Bill Laimbeer has coached three WNBA teams. Which of these teams has he NOT coached?

A. Detroit Shock

B. Las Vegas Aces

C. New York Liberty

D. Connecticut Sun

10. Through the 2021 season, who has played in the most games?

A. Candice DuPree

B. Sue Bird

C. Tamika Catchings

D. Tina Thompson

11. Through the 2021 season, what player has the highest single season scoring average?

A. Liz Cambage

B. Diana Taurasi

C. Maya Moore

D. Cynthia Cooper

12. As of the 2021 season, how many teams make up the WNBA?

A. 10

B. 12

C. 13

D. 14

13. This person was a three-time WNBA Coach of the Year.

A. Rick Mahorn

B. Cheryl Miller

C. Van Chancellor

D. Mike Thibault

14. Who was the first draft pick in the initial WNBA draft?

   A. Tina Thompson

   B. Sue Bird

   C. Pamela McGee

   D. Eva Nemcova

15. Through the 2021 season, who has the highest career scoring average?

   A. Diana Taurasi

   B. Cynthia Cooper

   C. Elena Delle Donna

   D. Breanna Stewart

16. Who is the all-time leading scorer for the New York Liberty?

    A. Cappie Pondexter

    B. Vicky Johnson

    C. Tina Charles

    D. Becky Hammon

17. This person was the first coach of the Phoenix Mercury.

    A. Jennifer Gillom

    B. Cheryl Miller

    C. Ron Rothstein

    D. Heidi VanDerveer

18. Which team has made the most playoff appearances?

    A. Las Vegas Aces

    B. Los Angeles Sparks

C. Seattle Storm

D. Phoenix Mercury

19. Who was the first pick of the 2021 WNBA draft?

   A. Charli Collier

   B. Chelsea Dungee

   C. Awal Kuier

   D. Aari McDonald

20. This first pick of 2013 WNBA draft has been a seven-time All-Star center for the Phoenix Mercury.

   A. Cappie Pondexter

   B. Brittney Griner

   C. Jennifer Gillom

   D. Maria Stepanova

21. Through the 2021 season, this coach is the all-time leader in wins for the Washington Mystics.

    A. Mike Thibault

    B. Tree Rollins

    C. Julie Plank

    D. Richie Adubato

22. Through the 2021 season, who is the all-time leading rebounder?

    A. Sylvia Fowles

    B. Tina Charles

    C. Candice Dupree

    D. Candace Parker

23. This coach led the Los Angeles Sparks to consecutive championships in 2001 and 2002.

    A. Michael Cooper

B. Kurt Rambis

C. Magic Johnson

D. Bob McAdoo

24. This player has the highest career scoring average for the Atlanta Dream.

A. Erika de Souza

B. Sancho Lyttle

C. Angel McCoughtry

D. Tiffany Hayes

25. Trough the 2021 season, this coach has the most victories in Chicago Sky franchise history.

A. James Wade

B. Steven Key

C. Pokey Chatman

D. Amber Stocks

26. Who is the all-time assists leader for the Las Vegas Aces franchise?

    A. Kelsey Plum

    B. Vicky Johnson

    C. Kayla McBride

    D. Becky Hammon

27. The Dallas Wings franchise began as this team.

    A. Detroit Red Wings

    B. Detroit Shock

    C. Tulsa Shock

    D. Fort Worth Red Wings

28. Through the 2021 season, this coach has the most wins in Minnesota Lynx franchise history.

    A. Don Zierden

    B. Brian Agler

    C. Cheryl Reeve

    D. Carolyn Jenkins

29. Liz Cambage holds the record for most points scored in a WNBA game while playing for the Dallas Wings. How many points did she score?

    A. 45

    B. 50

    C. 53

    D. 56

30. Through the 2021 season, who is the all-time leading rebounder for the New York Liberty?

A. Sue Wicks

B. Vicky Johnson

C. Tina Charles

D. Tari Phillips

31. Through the 2021 season, who is the all-time leading scorer for the Indiana Fever?

A. Briann January

B. Tamika Catchings

C. Katie Douglas

D. Kelsey Mitchell

32. Through the 2021 season, who has the highest career rebounding average?

A. Tina Charles

B. Sylvia Fowles

C. Cheryl Ford

D. Lisa Leslie

33. Through the 2021 season, who is the all-time leading scorer for the Connecticut Sun?

A. Nykesha Sales

B. Asjha Jones

C. Taj McWilliams-Franklin

D. Katie Douglas

34. She has the highest all-time scoring average for the Chicago Sky.

A. Elena Delle Donne

B. Candice Dupree

C. Sylvia Fowles

D. Epiphanny Prince

35. Who is the all-time scoring leader for the Las Vegas Aces franchise?

    A. Sophia Young-Malcolm

    B. Becky Hammon

    C. Adrienne Goodson

    D. Kayla McBride

36. Through the 2021 season, who is the WNBA career leader in assists?

    A. Sue Bird

    B. Cappie Pondexter

    C. Diana Taurasi

    D. Ticha Penicheiro

37. This former Los Angeles Lakers and Denver Nuggets coach led the Phoenix Mercury to the WNBA title in 2007.

    A. Mike Dunleavy

B. Paul Westhead

C. Pat Riley

D. Mike D'Antoni

38. Through the 2021 season, this coach is the all-time career leader in wins for the Indiana Fever.

A. Brian Winters

B. Lin Dunn

C. Stephanie White

D. Pokey Chatman

39. Who is the all-time leading scorer for the Washington Mystics?

A. Chamique Holdsclaw

B. Alana Beard

C. Monique Currie

D. Nikki McCray

40. True or False. Maya Moore is he all-time leading scorer for the Minnesota Lynx.

41. This player has the highest career scoring average for the Tulsa Shock/Dallas Wings.

    A. Skylar Diggins-Smith

    B. Swin Cash

    C. Cheryl Ford

    D. Deanna Nolan

42. Through the 2021 season, who has the highest WNBA career assist average?

    A. Dawn Staley

    B. Sue Bird

    C. Courtney Vandersloot

D. Cynthia Cooper

43. The Connecticut Sun began as this team.

    A. Orlando Magic

    B. Rhode Island Roosters

    C. Orlando Miracle

    D. Spirits of St. Louis

44. Through the 2021 season, she has played 18 seasons and is a 12-time All-Star, all with the Seattle Storm.

    A. Jewell Lloyd

    B. Breanna Stewart

    C. Sue Bird

    D. Lauren Jackson

45. Name the team that won the first four championships.

A. New York Liberty

B. Houston Comets

C. Sacramento Monarchs

D. Portland Fire

46. Who is the all-time leader in coaching wins for the New York Liberty?

A. Richie Adubato

B. Bill Laimbeer

C. Pat Coyle

D. Nancy Darsch

47. She was a four-time WNBA champion and averaged 15.0 points per game during her 12-year career with the Houston Comets, Seattle Storm, and Tulsa Shock.

A. Tamika Catchings

B. Ebony Hoffman

C. Sheryl Swoopes

D. Natalie Williams

48. True or False. Joe Bryant, Kobe Bryant's dad, once coached the Los Angeles Sparks.

49. The Las Vegas Aces began as this team.

    A. Utah Starzz

    B. Utah Stars

    C. Hollywood Starzz

    D. San Antonio Silver Stars

50. True or False. By 2009, after winning multiple championships, the Houston Comets were no longer in the league.

Answers

1. The inaugural season of the WNBA was in 1997.

2. There were eight teams that competed in the first WNBA season.

3. False. The first WNBA season had a 28-game regular season schedule.

4. The Houston comets won the first WNBA title in 1997.

5. Cynthia Cooper of the Houston rockets was the first league MVP.

6. Through the 2021 season, Diana Taurasi is the all-time leading scorer with 9,174 career points.

7. The Washington Mystics franchise began in the WNBA's second season.

8. Nancy Lieberman appeared in one game for the Detroit Shock in 2008 when she was 49 years old.

9. Bill Laimbeer never coached the Connecticut Sun.

10. Through the 2021 season, Sue Bird is the all-time leader in games played with 549.

11. Diana Taurasi has the highest single season scoring average when she scored 25.3 points per game in 2006 with the Phoenix Mercury.

12. There are currently 12 teams in the WNBA.

13. Van Chancellor was a three-time Coach of the Year, winning in 1997, 1998, and 1999.

14. Tina Thomas of USC was the first player drafted in 1997 by the Houston Comets.

15. Cynthia Cooper has the highest career scoring average of any WNBA player at 21.0 points per game.

16. Tina Charles has the highest scoring average in New York Liberty history at 18.7 points per game.

17. All-time collegiate great at USC, Cheryl Miller coached the Phoenix Mercury for the first four years of the franchise.

18. The Los Angeles Sparks have reached the playoffs 20 times, most of any WNBA team.

19. Charli Collier of Texas was the first player chosen in the 2021 WNBA draft, selected by the Dallas Wings.

20. Brittney Griner of the Phoenix Mercury has averaged 17.7 points per game and 7.6 rebounds per game since joining the league in 2013.

21. Mike Thibault has 151 regular season wins over nine seasons with the Washington Mystics.

22. Sylvia Fowles has pulled down 3,712 rebounds in her career, most in WNBA history.

23. Former Los Angeles Lakers sixth man Michael Cooper coached the Los Angeles Sparks to consecutive championships in 2001 and 2002.

24. Angel McCoughtry has the highest career scoring average for the Atlanta Dream with 19.1 points per game.

25. Pokey Chatman has 106 wins for the Chicago Sky, most in franchise history.

26. Becky Hammon is the all-time assists record for the Las Vegas Aces with 1,133. She accomplished that feat while the franchise was in San Antonio and known as the Stars.

27. The Dallas Wings were originally the Detroit Shock and began play in 1998.

28. Carol Reeve has 267 career wins with the Minnesota Lynx, most in franchise history.

29. Liz Cambage scored 53 points for the Dallas Wings against the New York Liberty in 2018.

30. Tina Charles is the all-time leading rebounder for the New York Liberty with 1,723 rebounds.

31. Tamika Catchings is the all-time leading scorer for the Indiana Fever 7,380 points.

32. Sylvia Fowles has the highest career rebounding average in WNBA history with 9.8 rebounds per game.

33. Nykesha Sales scored 3,955 points for the Sun, most of any player in Connecticut franchise history.

34. Elena Delle Donne has the highest lifetime scoring average for the Chicago Sky with 20.5 points per game.

35. Sophia Young-Malcolm scored 4,300 points, most in Las Vegas Aces franchise history.

36. Sue Bird is the all-time WNBA career leader in assists with 3,048.

37. Former Los Angeles Lakers and Denver Nuggets coach Paul Westhead led the Phoenix Mercury to the 2007 WNBA title.

38. Lin Dunn is the all-time winningest coach for the Indiana Fever with 135 wins.

39. Alana Beard is the all-time leading scorer for the Washington Mystics with 3,128 points.

40. False. Seimone Augustus is the all-time leading scorer for the Minnesota Lynx with 5,881 points.

41. Skylar Diggins-Smith has the highest career scoring average for the Tulsa Shock/Dallas Wings franchise with 15.9 points per game.

42. Courtney Vandersloot has the highest WNBA career assists average with 6.66 assists per game.

43. The Connecticut Sun spent the first four years of the franchise as the Orlando Miracle.

44. Sue Bird has played her entire 18 seasons with the Seattle Storm.

45. The Houston Comets won the first four WNBA championships.

46. Former NBA coach Richie Adubato is the winningest coach in New York Liberty franchise history with exactly 100 wins.

47. Sheryl Swoopes played 10 seasons with the Houston Comets, winning four WNBA titles.

48. True. Joe "Jellybean" Bryant, Lobe Bryant's dad, coached the Los Angeles Sparks for the 2006 season, leading them to a 25-9 regular season record.

49. The Las Vegas Aces franchise began as the Utah Starzz.

50. True. Despite winning the first four WNBA championships, by 2009 nine the Houston Comets were no longer a WNBA franchise.

The College Game

Long before there were any professional leagues, basketball was played at the high school and college level. It wasn't until the 1960s before the NBA began to outpace the college game for interest among fans. Yet, college basketball remains immensely popular, as the annual popularity of the NCAA Basketball Tournament can attest. Companies lose millions in lack of productivity while employees split their focus between their job and the early rounds of March Madness.

Some college greats went on to have great professional careers, while others did not make the transition quite as well. Yet they remain stars at the collegiate level. There are legendary coaches at the college level too. Go ahead, test your knowledge about the history of college basketball.

1. When was the first college basketball game played?

   A. 1896

   B. 1898

   C. 1899

   D. 1905

2. What two schools participated in the first game?

   A. Harvard/Yale

   B. Princeton/NYU

   C. Chicago/Iowa

   D. Duke/North Carolina

3. How many total points were scored in that first game?

   A. 5

   B. 12

C. 27

D. 44

4. Who is the all-time leading scorer in NCAA college basketball history?

A. Oscar Robertson

B. Elvin Hayes

C. Lionel Simmons

D. Pete Maravich

5. The first NCAA college basketball tournament was held in 1939. Who was the first NCAA champion?

A. Texas

B. Ohio State

C. Oregon

D. Villanova

6. How many teams comprised the first NCAA college basketball tournament?

    A. 4

    B. 6

    C. 8

    D. 10

7. Through the 2020-2021 season, how many national championships has Indiana won?

    A. 2

    B. 4

    C. 5

    D. 6

8. Through the 2020-2021 season, how many Duke players have won Player of the Year award?

A. 5

B. 6

C. 7

D. 8

9. What year was the college basketball All-America team first named?

A. 1933-1934

B. 1940-1941

C. 1947-1948

D. 1955-1956

10. This Purdue sharpshooter was First team All-America for the 1968-1969 and 1969-1970 seasons.

A. John Roche

B. Rick Mount

C. Charlie Scott

D. Calvin Murphy

11. True or False. John Wooden's UCLA Bruins won seven consecutive NCAA national titles.

12. Name the school that was the first to have an all-black starting lineup?

A. San Francisco

B. Texas Western

C. Syracuse

D. Oregon

13. Who was the 1966 NCAA champion?

A. Kansas

B. Kentucky

C. Texas Western

D. Ohio State

14. Who was the first African American All-American college basketball player?

    A. Jackie Robinson

    B. Earl Lloyd

    C. George Gregory

    D. K.C. Jones

15. In 1951, the NCAA college basketball tournament expanded to how many teams?

    A. 12

    B. 16

    C. 20

    D. 24

16. True or False. Jim Boeheim has spent his entire coaching career art Syracuse.

17. Elgin Baylor played his college basketball at this school.

   A. Texas A & M

   B. Georgetown

   C. Seattle

   D. Oregon

18. He led Oklahoma A & M (now Oklahoma State) to back-to-back NCAA tournament championships in 1945 and 1946.

   A. Bob Kurland

   B. Arnie Ferrin

   C. Ken Sailors

   D. Jim Pollard

19. Through the 2020-2021 season, how many national titles has the University of Connecticut women's team won?

    A. 5

    B. 9

    C. 11

    D. 13

20. Through the 2020-2021 season, how many national titles has UConn's women's team won under head coach Geno Auriemma?

    A. 5

    B. 8

    C. 9

    D. 11

21. This player won back-to-back Player of the Year awards while at North Carolina State in 1974-1975.

A. Monte Towe

B. Tom Burleson

C. David Thompson

D. Scott May

22. Who was the first African American player to play at North Carolina?

A. Bob McAdoo

B. Walter Davis

C. Charlie Scott

D. Michael Jordon

23. Through the 2020-2021 season, what school has the most Final Four appearances?

A. Kansas

B. Duke

C. North Carolina

D. UCLA

24. This one-time member of the Original Celtics had two stints coaching St. Johns, 20 years total. He amassed a career winning percentage there of .720.

A. Red Klotz

B. Joe Lapchick

C. Lou Carnesecca

D. Nat Holman

25. Adolph Rupp coached at only one school. Name the school.

A. Kentucky

B. Kansas

C. Bowling Green

D. South Carolina

26. How many seasons did Adolph Rupp coach college basketball?

    A. 33

    B. 38

    C. 40

    D. 41

27. Wilt Chamberlain did not play his senior season at Kansas in 1958-1959. Instead, who did he play for?

    A. Philadelphia Tapers of the American Basketball League

    B. Philadelphia Warriors

    C. Temple

    D. Harlem Globetrotters

28. Through the 2020-2021 season, what school has the most NCAA tournament appearances?

A. Kentucky

B. North Carolina

C. Duke

D. Kansas

29. In the early years, the National Invitation Tournament (NIT) was bigger than the NCAA tournament. This future NBA great big man led DePaul to the NIT championship in 1945.

A. Arnie Risen

B. Nat Clifton

C. Vern Mikkelsen

D. George Mikan

30. Through the 2020-2021 season, which women's college basketball coach is the all-time leader in career wins?

A. Geno Auriemma

B. Tara VanDerveer

C. Pat Summit

D. Vivian Stringer

31. What year did UCLA make its first NCAA tournament appearance?

    A. 1948

    B. 1950

    C. 1955

    D. 1960

32. True or False. Through the 2020-2021 season, North Carolina has appeared in the NCAA tournament 50 times.

33. Alex Groza was named Most Outstanding Player of the NCAA tournament in 1948 and 1949, playing for the eventual champion. What school did he play for?

A. Louisville

B. Kentucky

C. Florida

D. St. Johns

34. The NCAA college basketball tournament grew to how many teams in 1975?

A. 32

B. 36

C. 40

D. 52

35. Through the 2020-2021 season, how many national championships has Villanova won?

A. 1

B. 3

C. 4

D. 5

36. Although his Kansas team lost to North Carolina in the NCAA championship game in 1967, this player was named the tournament's Most Outstanding Player.

A. Tom Gola

B. Wilt Chamberlain

C. K.C. Jones

D. Hal Lear

37. The Associated Press Women's College Basketball Player of the Year award was established in 1995. Through the 2020-2021 season, how many times has a player from UConn won the award?

A. 8

B. 10

C. 12

D. 14

38. Who was the first Women's Player of the Year in 1995?

A. Rebecca Lobo

B. Jennifer Rizzotti

C. Kara Wolters

D. Ruth Riley

39. This school holds the unique record of winning both the NIT championship and the NCAA championship in the same season.

A. Dayton

B. City College of New York

C. Kentucky

D. Florida State

40. Through the 2020-2021 season, which coach has the most wins in college basketball history?

A. Mike Krzyzewski

B. Jim Boeheim

C. Dean Smith

D. Bob Huggins

41. This Indiana State star was named the AP Player of the Year in 1979.

A. Magic Johnson

B. Joe Barry Carroll

C. Larry Bird

D. Bill Cartwright

42. Future Boston Celtics teammates Bill Russell and K.C. Jones led this school to two consecutive NCAA championships in 1955 and 1956.

A. Boston College

B. San Francisco

C. California

D. Holy Cross

43. Through the 2020-2021 season, how many national championships has North Carolina won?

A. 4

B. 6

C. 8

D. 9

44. In 1985, the NCAA college basketball tournament expanded to how many teams?

A. 32

B. 44

C. 52

D. 64

45. Through the 2020-2021 season, how many Final Four appearances does UCLA have?

A. 13

B. 14

C. 18

D. 20

46. How many wins did Bobby Knight have when he finished his career?

A. 850

B. 875

C. 899

D. 900

47. This player, known as "Hot Rod" was a star at West Virginia from 1954-1957, averaging 24.5 points per game. He later played for the Los Angele Lakers.

A. Jerry West

B. Rod Thorn

C. Rod Hundley

D. Rodney Rogers

48. Who is the all-time leading scorer in women's college basketball?

A. Cheryl Miller

B. Jackie Stiles

C. Kelsey Plum

D. Kelsey Mitchell

49. Pat Summitt coached the women's basketball team at this school for 38 years.

A. Arkansas

B. Tennessee

C. Mississippi State

D. Kentucky

50. How many wins did Pat Summitt amass in her career?

A. 1050

B. 1075

C. 1098

D. 1100

51. Through the 2020-2021 season, how many Final Four appearances does Duke have?

A. 10

B. 16

C. 18

D. 19

52. Jerry Lucas was named back-to-back Most Outstanding Player in the 1960 and 1961 NCAA tournaments. What school did he help lead to the NCAA championship in 1960?

A. Michigan

B. Providence

C. Ohio State

D. Penn State

53. This player was named the Sporting News Player of the Year in 1958, 1959, and 1960.

A. Terry Dischinger

B. Oscar Robertson

C. Jerry Lucas

D. Bob Boozer

54. Through the 2020-2021 season, how many national championships has Kansas won?

A. 1

B. 3

C. 5

D. 7

55. This player was a three-time Women's College Basketball Player of the Year from 2014-2016.

A. Kelsey Plum

B. A'ja Wilson

C. Breanna Stewart

D. Brittny Griner

56. This LSU star was First Team All-America for three consecutive seasons, 1967-1968, 1968-1969, and 1969-1970.

A. Elvin Hayes

B. Wes Unseld

C. Pete Maravich

D. Neal Walk

57. Through the 2020-2021 season, how many NCAA tournament appearances has Kansas made?

A. 43

B. 48

C. 49

D. 52

58. The 1964-1965 All-America Teams included three players who would be teammates on the New York Knicks

1969-1970 NBA championship team. One of these players would not.

A. Dave Stallworth

B. Cazzie Russell

C. Fred Hetzel

D. Bill Bradley

59. What year did John Wooden first start coaching at UCLA?

A. 1944-1945

B. 1948-1949

C. 1955-1956

D. 1960-1961

60. In a foreshadowing of their NBA careers, these two players met in the NCAA Finals in 1979.

A. Julius Erving/Larry Bird

B. Larry Bird/Magic Johnson

C. Wilt Chamberlain/Bill Russell

D. Jerry West/Oscar Robertson

61. They were members of Kentucky's "Fabulous Five" championship teams in 1947-1948 and 1948-1949 as well as first or second team All-America those same seasons. After two seasons in the NBA, they were banned for life for their involvement in a point shaving scandal while at Kentucky.

A. Wah Wah Jones/Adoph Rupp

B. Ralph Beard/Wah Wah Jones

C. Alex Groza/Ralph Beard

D. Alex Groza/Lou Groza

62. Since the NCAA tournament expanded in 1985, Virginia became the first number 1 seed to lose to a number 16 seed in the first round. Who beat them?

A. Loyola Marymount

B. Grand Canyon University

C. University of Maryland-Baltimore County

D. New Mexico State

63. Through the 2020-2021 season, how many Final Four appearances does Villanova have?

    A. 2

    B. 4

    C. 5

    D. 6

64. Vivian Stringer has coached women's college basketball for 50 seasons. She has coached at all but one of these schools.

    A. Cheyney

    B. Iowa

    C. Rutgers

D. St. Johns

65. Through the 2020-2021 season, how many national championships has Duke won?

A. 2

B. 3

C. 5

D. 6

66. True or False. Lew Alcindor, later Kareem Abdul-Jabber, was named the Most Outstanding Player of the NCAA tournament three straight years, from 1967-1969.

67. How many times did John Wooden's UCLA Bruins finish the season undefeated?

A. 1

B. 2

C. 3

D. 4

68. The 1957-1958 All-America teams included three players who would later team up with the Lakers team that battled the Boston Celtics in the 1968-1969 NBA Finals. One of these players would not.

A. Wilt Chamberlain

B. Baily Howell

C. Jerry West

D. Elgin Baylor

69. Name the player who has scored the most points in an NCAA tournament career.

A. Elvin Hayes

B. Christian Laettner

C. Oscar Robertson

D. Danny Manning

70. Through the 2020-2021 season, how many Final Four appearances does Indiana have?

A. 4

B. 6

C. 8

D. 10

71. True or False. Through the 2020-2021 season, UCLA has appeared in 48 NCAA tournaments.

72. This Los Angeles Lakers great starred at West Virginia from 1957-1960, averaging 24.8 points per game, before moving on to the Los Angeles Lakers.

A. Rod Thorn

B. Rod Hundley

C. Jerry West

D. Jerry Stackhouse

73. How many seasons did Dean Smith coach at North Carolina?

    A. 25

    B. 28

    C. 33

    D. 36

74. Who holds the record for the most points in an NCAA tournament game?

    A. Bill Bradley

    B. Austin Carr

    C. David Robinson

    D. Oscar Robertson

75. What year did Duke first appear in the NCAA tournament?

    A. 1940

    B. 1945

    C. 1950

    D. 1955

76. Which coach has the most NCAA tournament wins?

    A. Mike Krzyzewski

    B. Bob Knight

    C. John Wooden

    D. Dean Smith

77. True or False. Prior to coaching at Gonzaga, Mark Few was head coach at Long Beach State.

78. This player led Georgetown to the NCAA championship in 1984.

    A. David Wingate

    B. Sleepy Floyd

    C. Patrick Ewing

    D. Dikembe Mutombo

79. Through the 2020-2021 season, how many times has UCLA won the national championship?

    A. 8

    B. 9

    C. 10

    D. 11

80. The 1955-1956 All-America team included three future Boston Celtics. One of these never played for the Celtics.

    A. Bill Russell

B. Tom Heinsohn

C. K.C. Jones

D. Lenny Rosenbluth

81. This Second Team 1983-1984 All-America player would later go on to become an NBA referee, following a seven-year NBA career as a player.

A. Leon Wood

B. Sam Bowie

C. Michael Cage

D. Keith Lee

82. This mid-major university from Indiana played in back-to-back NCAA championship games in 2010 and 2011.

A. Indiana State

B. Butler

C. Valparaiso

D. DePauw

83. In his one season at Mississippi in 1970-1971, this player averaged 40.1 points per game.

A. Johnny Neumann

B. Coolidge Ball

C. Fred Cox

D. Ansu Sesay

84. This player holds the NCAA record for most points in one game with 100.

A. Wilt Chamberlain

B. Frank Selvy

C. Bo Kimble

D. Tom Gola

85. Name the player who holds the all-time single season record highest rebounds per game average.

A. Artis Gilmore

B. Bill Russell

C. Paul Silas

D. Charlie Slack

86. Phog Allen spent 37 seasons, collecting 809 of his total 978 wins, coaching at this school.

A. North Carolina

B. Kansas

C. South Carolina

D. Oregon State

87. This school upset the heavily favored Georgetown Hoyas in the 1985 NCAA championship game, shooting 79% from the field in the game.

A. St. Johns

B. Villanova

C. Memphis

D. Duke

88. This First Team All-America from Indiana later became a college coach with stops at UCLA, New Mexico, and Iowa, among others.

A. Scott Skiles

B. Danny Manning

C. Steve Alford

D. William Bedford

89. True or False. UCLA holds the record for most consecutive wins with 76.

90. This player led the nation in scoring three consecutive seasons in scoring, including an NCAA record 44.5 points per game in 1969-1970.

A. Johnny Neumann

B. Pete Maravich

C. Lew Alcindor

D. Kurt Thomas

91. This Temple Owl once scored 54 consecutive points in a game.

A. Bill Mlkvy

B. Michael Jordon

C. Bill Walton

D. Larry Bird

92. This coached amassed 1,085 wins in his career that spanned from 1929-1970, including 36 seasons with Oklahoma State.

A. Hank Iba

B. Slats Gil

C. Hugh Durham

D. Guy Lewis

93. The 1949-1950 All-America team included three future Boston Celtics. One of these never played for the Celtics.

A. Clyde Lovellette

B. Bob Cousy

C. Bill Sharman

D. Whitey Skoog

94. Jerry Tarkanian coached this school to the national championship in 1990.

A. Fresno State

B. UNLV

C. Cal-State Long Beach

D. USC

95. True or False. Arizona has never won the national championship.

96. This UConn star won the Women's College Basketball Player of the Year in 2003.

A. Diana Taurasi

B. Sue Bird

C. Maya Moore

D. Tina Charles

97. Before coaching at North Carolina, Roy Williams coached 15 seasons at this school.

A. Kansas

B. Kansas State

C. Nebraska

D. Oklahoma State

98. This Virginia star won three consecutive Player of the Year awards from 1981-1983.

    A. Hakeem Olajuwon

    B. Ralph Sampson

    C. Scott May

    D. Hersey Hawkins

99. Through the 2020-2021 season, how many times has Kentucky won the national championship?

    A. 6

    B. 8

C. 10

D. 12

100. Sandwiched in between Lew Alcindor and Bill Walton, this player was UCLA's starting center on back-to-back national championship teams.

    A. Sydney Wicks

    B. Steve Patterson

    C. Swen Nater

    D. Curtis Rowe

Answers

1. The first college basketball game was played in 1896.

2. The first college game featured the University of Chicago and Iowa.

3. Twenty-seven points were scored in that initial game as Chicago defeated Iowa 15-12.

4. LSU's Pete Maravich is the all-time leading scorer in NCAA college basketball history with 3,667 career points.

5. Oregon defeated Ohio State 46-33 to claim the first NCAA tournament championship in 1939.

6. The first NCAA tournament consisted of eight teams.

7. Indiana has won five national championships.

8. Duke players have won seven Payer of the Year awards.

9. The All-America team was first named following the 1947-1948 season.

10. Purdue's Rick Mount was First Team All-America for the 1968-1969 and 1969-1970 seasons.

11. True. Under John Wooden, UCLA won seven consecutive NCAA championships from 1967-1973.

12. Texas Western (Now UTEP) started an all-black starting lineup in the 1966 NCAA championship game against Kentucky.

13. Texas Western defeated Kentucky 72-65 to claim the 1966 championship.

14. George Gregory, captain and center of the Columbia University team from 1928-1931 became the first African American All-American college basketball player in 1931.

15. In 1951, the NCAA tournament was expanded to 16 teams.

16. True. Jim Boeheim began his head coaching career with Syracuse in 1976 and has continued through the 2021-2022 season, all with Syracuse.

17. Elgin Baylor starred at Seattle University in college.

18. Bob Kurland led Oklahoma A & M to back-to-back NCAA tournament championships in 1945 and 1946.

19. UConn's women's team has won 11 national championships.

20. UConn's women's team won all 11 of its national championships under head coach Geno Auriemma.

21. North Carolina State's David Thompson won the Player of the Year award for 1974 and 1975.

22. Charlie Scott was the first African American to play at North Carolina for the 1966-1967 season.

23. North Carolina has made 20 Final Four appearances through the 2020-20231 season.

24. Joe Lapchick coached St. Johns from 1936-1947 and again from 1956-1965, amassing 334 wins and a .720 winning percentage.

25. Adolph Rupp coached only at Kentucky, winning 876 games.

26. Adolph Rupp coached at Kentucky from 1930-1971, 41 seasons.

27. Rather than play his senior season with Kansas, Wilt Chamberlain chose to play with the Harlem Globetrotters.

28. Kentucky has 58 NCAA tournament appearances through the 2020-2021 season.

29. George Mikan led DePaul to the 1945 NIT championship.

30. Through the 2020-2021 season, Tara VanDerveer has won 1,143 games, mostly at Stanford.

31. UCLA made its first NCAA tournament appearance in 1950.

32. False. Through the 2020-2021 season, North Carolina has made 51 NCAA tournament appearances.

33. Alex Groza played at Kentucky.

34. The NCAA tournament expanded to 32 teams in 1975.

35. Villanova has won three national championships.

36. Wilt Chamberlain was the 1957 NCAA tournament Most Outstanding Player.

37. Through the 2020-2021 season UConn players have won the Associated Press Women's College Basketball Player of the Year award.

38. UConn's Rebecca Lobo was the first Women's Player of the Year in 1995.

39. City College of New York (CCNY) won both the NIT championship and the NCAA championship in 1950.

40. Through the 2020-2021 season, Duke's Mike Krzyzewski has won 1,170 games.

41. Indiana State's Larry Bird was the AP Player of the Year in 1979.

42. Bill Russell and K.C. Jones led San Francisco to championships in 1955 and 1956.

43. North Carolina has won six national championships through the 2020-2021 season.

44. The NCAA tournament expanded to 64 teams in 1985.

45. UCLA has appeared in 18 Final Fours.

46. Bobby Knight won 902 wins in his coaching career.

47. "Hot Rod" Hundley starred at West Virginia from 1954-1957.

48. Washington's Kelsey Plum is the all-time leading scorer in women's college basketball with 3,527 career points.

49. Pat Summitt coached the Lady Vols at Tennessee from 1974-2012.

50. Pat Summitt won 1,098 games in her career

51. Duke has 16 Final Four appearances through the 2020-2021 season.

52. Jerry Lucas helped lead Ohio State to the 1960 NCAA championship in 1960.

53. Cincinnati's Oscar Robertson was the Sporting News Player of the Year in 1958, 1959, and 1960.

54. Kansas has won three national championships.

55. UConn's Breanna Stewart won the Women's College Basketball Player of the Year from 2014-2016.

56. LSU's Pete Maravich was First Team All-America for the 1967-1968, 1968-1969, and 1969-1970 seasons.

57. Kansas has made 49 NCAA tournament appearances.

58. Dave Stallworth, Cazzie Russell, and Bill Bradley were all members of the New York Knicks NBA championship team in 1969-1970.

59. John Wooden first started coaching at UCLA in 1948.

60. Larry Bird led Indiana State into the championship game against Magic Johnson's Michigan State team. Michigan State won 75-64.

61. Kentucky's Alex Groza and Ralph Beard were implicated in a point shaving scandal. Although it took place during their college careers, they were not implicated until they had been in the NBA for two years. Following their admissions of guilt, both were banned from the NBA for life.

62. UMBC defeated Virginia 74-54 in 2018, becoming the first number 16 seed to defeat a number 1 seed in the first round.

63. Villanova has made five Final Four appearances.

64. Vivian Stringer has never coached at St. Johns.

65. Duke has won five national championships.

66. True. Lew Alcindor was the Most Outstanding Player of the NCAA tournament from 1967-1969.

67. UCLA had four undefeated seasons under John Wooden.

68. Wilt Chamberlain, Elgin Baylor, and Jerry West all played for the Los Angeles Lakers in the 1968-1969 NBA Finals.

69. Christian Laettner is the all-time leading scorer in NCAA tournament history with 407 points.

70. Indiana has made 8 Final Four appearances.

71. True. UCLA has appeared in 48 NCAA tournaments.

72. Jerry West followed "Hot Rod" Hundley to West Virginia and then to the Lakers.

73. Dean Smith coached North Carolina for 36 seasons.

74. Austin Carr of Notre Dame poured in 61 points against Ohio in 1970.

75. Duke's first NCAA tournament appearance was in 1955.

76. Through the 2020-2021 season Mike Krzyzewski has 97 NCAA tournament wins, the most in history.

77. False. Mark Few was not a head coach at any other school prior to taking the job at Gonzaga.

78. Patrick Ewing led the Georgetown Hoyas to the national championship in 1984.

79. UCLA has won 11 national championships.

80. Bill Russell, Tom Heinsohn, and K.C. Jones were All-Americans in 1955-1956 and later were teammates with the Boston Celtics.

81. Leon Wood was a second team All-American in 1983-1984, played in the NBA for six years and has been a referee for over 25 years.

82. Butler played in back-to-back national championship games, losing to Duke in 2010 and Connecticut in 2011.

83. Johnny Neumann played one season at Ole Miss, averaging 40.1 points per game, before leaving for the ABA.

84. Frank Selvy of Furman scored 100 points against Newberry in 1954.

85. Charlie Slack of Marshall average 25.6 rebounds per game in 1954-1955.

86. Phog Allen coached from 1919-1956 at Kansas.

87. Villanova upset Georgetown 66-64, making 22 of 28 shots.

88. Steve Alford was an All-American, who later coached at Iowa, New Mexico, UCLA, and Nevada.

89. False. UCLA holds the record with 88 consecutive wins from 1972-1974.

90. Pete Maravich of LSU led the nation in scoring from his sophomore season through his senior season.

91. Bill Mlkvy of Temple scored 54 consecutive points against Wilkes College in 1951.

92. Hank Iba coached at Oklahoma State for 36 seasons.

93. All-American Whitey Skoog never played for the Boston Celtics.

94. Jerry Tarkanian led the UNLV Rebels to the 1990 NCAA championship.

95. False. Arizona won the national championship in 1997.

96. UConn's Diana Taurasi was the 2003 Women's Player of the Year.

97. Roy Williams coached at Kansas prior to North Carolina.

98. Ralph Sampson was Player of the Year from 1981-1983.

99. Kentucky has won eight national championships.

100. Steve Patterson was UCLA's starting center between Lew Alcindor and Bill Walton.

Hall of Fame

The Basketball Hall of Fame celebrates the history of the game from its inception to today. Hall of Fame inductees include star players, both professional and collegiate, as well as players from early barnstorming teams. All-time great professional and college coaches, contributors, and even referees are also members of the Hall of Fame.

Find out how much you know about the members of the Basketball Hall of Fame.

1. The Basketball Hall of Fame is named after this individual.

A. Larry Bird

B. Larry O'Brien

C. James Naismith

D. David Stern

2. Where is the Hall of Fame located?

  A. Cooperstown, NY

  B. Springfield, MA

  C. Canton, OH

  D. Providence, RI

3. He was the first individual to have a basketball shoe named after him.

  A. Bob Cousy

  B. Michael Jordon

  C. Julius Erving

  D. Chuck Taylor

4. What year was the first Hall of Fame class inducted?

    A. 1959

    B. 1960

    C. 1968

    D. 1970

5. This entire team was inducted into the Hall of Fame in the first class.

    A. Harlem Globetrotters

    B. New York Rens

    C. Original Celtics

    D. Phillips 66ers

6. This center for DePaul and the Minneapolis Lakers was also part of the first Hall of Fame class.

    A. George Mikan

B. Joe Lapchick

C. Vern Mikkelsen

D. Bud Grant

7. He was inducted into the Hall of Fame as a player in 1960 and as a coach in 1973.

　　A. Red Auerbach

　　B. John Wooden

　　C. Alex Hannum

　　D. Nat Holman

8. He led the Montana State Golden Bobcats to a 102-11 record in three seasons (1927-1930), averaging 15.4 points per game at a time when teams routinely scored around 40 points a game.

　　A. Joe Lapchick

　　B. John "Cat" Thompson

C. Bob Kurland

D. John Schommer

9. This Duquesne All-American was the first African American to be drafted by an NBA team.

A. Chuck Cooper

B. Nat Clifton

C. Earl Lloyd

D. Curl Neal

10. He starred for the Virginia Squires and New York Nets in the ABA and the Philadelphia 76ers in the NBA.

A. George McGinnis

B. Billy Cunningham

C. Julius Erving

D. Larry Kenon

11. This entire team from 1966 was inducted into the Hall of Fame after becoming the first school to start an all-black lineup.

A. NYCC

B. Kentucky

C. Texas Western

D. St. Johns

12. He was the first person to simultaneously be the commissioner of the National Basketball Association and president of the American Hockey League.

A. Maurice Podoloff

B. Walter Kennedy

C. David Stern

D. Larry O'Brien

13. This two-time All-American led Kentucky to the 1951 NCAA championship and also won seven NBA championships with the Boston Celtics.

A. Bob Cousy

B. K.C. Jones

C. Frank Ramsey

D. Tom "Satch" Sanders

14. He was both a player and a coach for the Houston Rockets.

A. Calvin Murphy

B. Rudy Tomjanovich

C. Alex Hannum

D. Clyde Drexler

15. Known as "the Jet," this player starred with both the Syracuse Nationals/Philadelphia 76ers and the Chicago Bulls.

    A. Lucious Jackson

    B. Dolph Schayes

    C. Bill Melchionni

    D. Chet Walker

16. This former LSU star was the NBA Rookie of the Year and also two-time MVP with the St. Louis Hawks.

    A. Cliff Hagen

    B. Lenny Wilkens

    C. Bob Pettit

    D. Slater Martin

17. He led UCLA to an 88-game winning streak and two NCAA championships, making 21 of 22 shots in the 1973 NCAA championship game.

    A. Keith Wiles

    B. Curtis Rowe

    C. Bill Walton

    D. Henry Bibby

18. After his collegiate career at Navy, he went on to be a 10-time NBA All-Star and once scored 71 points in a game for the San Antonio Spurs.

    A. David Robinson

    B. Tim Duncan

    C. George Gervin

    D. Sean Elliott

19. In one 13-month stretch from 1956-1957, this player won the NCAA championship, an Olympic gold medal, and the NBA championship.

   A. K.C. Jones

   B. Bill Russell

   C. Oscar Robertson

   D. George Mikan

20. She led Old Dominion University in back-to-back AIAW national championships in 1979 and 1980.

   A. Cheryl Miller

   B. Nancy Lieberman

   C. Diana Taurasi

   D. Rebecca Lobo

21. This power forward was a key component of the Baltimore Bullets of the mid-1960s and early 1970s,

including reaching the 1971 NBA Finals and finally winning a championship in 1973 with the ABA Indiana Pacers.

A. Gus Johnson

B. Jack Marin

C. Kevin Loughery

D. Wes Unseld

22. This player nicknamed the "Big O" played for Cincinnati in college and in the NBA.

A. Jermaine O'Neal

B. Oscar Robertson

C. Shaquille O'Neal

D. Tom Owens

23. He won an NCAA championship with Ohio State and eight NBA championships with the Boston Celtics.

A. Bill Sharman

B. Dave Cowens

C. Cedric Maxwell

D. John Havlicek

24. He led Long Island University to two NIT championships in 1939 and 1941 and was credited with inventing the 1-3-1 defense.

A. Hank Iba

B. Rick Pitino

C. Clair Bee

D. Pat Riley

25. Through the 2020-2021 season, this player is second all-time in assists in the NBA.

A. Magic Johnson

B. Jason Kidd

C. Mark Jackson

D. Steve Nash

26. She was a four-time Olympic Gold Medalist and led Tennessee to the NCAA Women's championship in 1998. Her father also played in the NBA.

    A. Cheryl Miller

    B. Tamika Catchings

    C. Chamique Holdsclaw

    D. Candace Parker

27. This former Stanford standout became the first player in NBA history to score 2,000 points in one season (2,001) in 1957-1958.

    A. George Mikan

    B. Bill Sharman

    C. George Yardley

    D. Bob Pettit

28. This Indiana Pacers guard was one of the great players in the ABA, helping the Pacers win three ABA championships.

    A. Roger Brown

    B. Mel Daniels

    C. Larry Brown

    D. Doug Moe

29. True or False. Magic Johnson is the Los Angeles Lakers all-time leader in assists.

30. Playing for six NBA teams, this former Georgetown Hoya was a six-time member of the NBA's All-Defensive Team. He played 18 professional seasons and retired second on the NBA's career blocked shots list.

    A. Patrick Ewing

    B. Mark Eaton

    C. Nate Thurmond

D. Dikembe Mutombo

31. He was the 1967-1968 ABA MVP with the Pittsburgh Pipers and a 1969-1970 First Team All-NBA performer with the Phoenix Suns.

    A. Paul Silas

    B. Connie Hawkins

    C. Dick Van Arsdale

    D. Charlie Scott

32. His nickname was "Easy Ed" during his 10-year NBA career and was named MVP of the first NBA All-Star game in 1951.

    A. Ed Pickney

    B. Ed Macauley

    C. Ed Manning

    D. Eddie Miles

33. After averaging over 33 points per game for Niagara, this 5'9" guard starred for 13 seasons with the San Diego/Houston Rockets.

    A. Kenny Smith

    B. John Lucas

    C. Calvin Murphy

    D. Mario Ellie

34. He starred with Denver in the ABA and five NBA teams. His lawsuit against the NBA paved the way for players to turn professional before their four years of college were completed.

    A. Phil Chenier

    B. Spencer Haywood

    C. Moses Malone

    D. Johnny Neumann

35. He was a two-time NBA Finals MVP with the New York Knicks.

    A. Walt Frasier

    B. Bill Bradley

    C. Earl Monroe

    D. Willis Reed

36. While coaching at North Carolina, he devised the four-corners offense to slow the game down when his team had a lead.

    A. Roy Williams

    B. Dean Smith

    C. Phog Allen

    D. James Naismith

37. He was a six-time All-Star with New York Knicks (1958-1963) and was later player-coach of the Atlanta Hawks.

A. Red Holzman

B. Lenny Wilkins

C. Carl Braun

D. Richie Guerin

38. He was the first modern player to go straight from high school to professional basketball, starting with the ABA's Utah Stars and later playing 12 NBA All-Star seasons, primarily with the Houston Rockets and the Philadelphia 76ers.

A. Moses Malone

B. Bobby Dandridge

C. Jermaine O'Neal

D. Kevin Garnett

39. She won two WNBA championships with the Los Angeles Sparks and was a three-time WNBA MVP.

A. Diana Taurasi

B. Val Ackerman

C. Teresa Weatherspoon

D. Lisa Leslie

40. He had a 14-year playing career and a coaching career that spanned more than 30 years; he has been involved in more than 3,700 NBA games.

A. Phil Jackson

B. Don Nelson

C. Red Holzman

D. Jerry Sloan

41. This small forward teamed with Michael Jordon at North Carolina and Magic Johnson with the Los Angeles Lakers.

A. Michael Cooper

B. Norm Nixon

C. James Worthy

D. Kurt Rambis

42. He is one of only three coaches in history to win the triple crown: an NIT, NCAA, and Olympic title.

A. Pete Newell

B. Adolph Rupp

C. Dean Smith

D. Mark Few

43. After a brief NBA career backing up Bill Russell, he went on to a stellar college coaching career with Georgetown.

A. Patrick Ewing

B. John Thompson

C. Henry Finkle

D. Eric "Sleepy" Floyd

44. In 1968, he became the youngest general manager in professional sports when he took over the expansion Phoenix Suns at 28 years old.

A. Johnny Kerr

B. Alex Hannum

C. Jerry Colangelo

D. Al Bianchi

45. He was the owner of NBL's Fort Wayne Zollner Pistons (1941-48), later the Fort Wayne Pistons of the NBA (1948-49, NBA: 1949-57), and finally the NBA's Detroit Pistons (1957-1974).

A. Jerry Buss

B. Fred Zollner

C. Charlie Finley

D. Abe Saperstein

46. He was nicknamed "Harrisburg Houdini" and led the Rochester Royals to the NBA title in 1949-1950.

A. Bob Davies

B. Red Holzman

C. Arnie Risen

D. Bobby Wanzer

47. Known as "Lefty" he coached for 41 seasons at Davidson, Maryland, James Madison, and Georgia State.

A. Luther Gulick

B. Bernard Carnevale

C. Charles Driesell

D. Ward Lambert

48. He led Arkansas to the Final Four in 1978 and was the recipient of the first NBA Defensive Player of the Year award in 1983, while with the Milwaukee Bucks.

A. Dennis Johnson

B. Sidney Moncrief

C. Elvin Hayes

D. Ron Harper

49. He won back-to-back NCAA national championships with San Francisco and eight NBA championships with the Boston Celtics.

A. Frank Ramsey

B. John Havlicek

C. K.C. Jones

D. Sam Jones

50. True or False. Pat Summitt coached the Tennessee Lady Vols to 22 Final Fours.

51. This defensive standout was named to eight straight NBA All-Defense First Team honors while playing for the Denver Nuggets and Philadelphia 76ers.

   A. George McGinnis

   B. Dan Issel

   C. T.R. Dunn

   D. Bobby Jones

52. After winning three consecutive NBA titles, he left the game to try baseball. Once he returned to the NBA, he won three more consecutive NBA titles.

   A. Dave DeBusschere

   B. Michael Jordon

   C. Danny Ainge

   D. Norm Nixon

53. He is the Los Angeles Lakers all-time leading scorer.

A. Jerry West

B. Kareem Abdul-Jabbar

C. Kobe Bryant

D. Elgin Baylor

54. He played 14 seasons in the NBA and was the Rookie of the Year in 1961-1962 after averaging 31.6 points and 19.0 rebounds per game.

A. Terry Dischinger

B. Walt Bellamy

C. Zelmo Beatty

D. Bob Pettit

55. During her career at UCLA, she was the first player, male or female, named to the All-America team in four straight seasons.

A. Lisa Leslie

B. Anne Donavan

C. Ann Meyers-Drysdale

D. Bertha Teague

56. Intense and with a volatile temper, he coached collegiately for 42 seasons, including leading Indiana to a perfect 32-0 season in 1976.

A. Tom Izzo

B. Bobby Knight

C. Hank Iba

D. Rick Pitino

57. After a stellar career at Kentucky, he played nine seasons in the NBA and then coached the Los Angeles Lakers, New York Knicks, and Miami Heat, winning five NBA championships.

A. Jack Ramsey

B. Pat Riley

C. Billy Cunningham

D. Phil Jackson

58. An undersized center, he played 11 seasons in the NBA and won two NBA titles with Boston in 1974 and 1976.

A. Bill Russell

B. Robert Parish

C. Dave Cowens

D. Henry Finkle

59. Playing his entire career with one franchise, he led the Syracuse Nationals/Philadelphia 76ers to playoff berths 15 times in his 16-year career.

A. Dolph Schayes

B. Hal Greer

C. Johnny "Red" Kerr

D. Harry Gallatin

60. He coached four teams, Philadelphia 76ers, Buffalo Braves, Portland Trailblazers, and Indiana Pacers during his 21-year NBA coaching career.

A. Gene Shue

B. Kevin Loughery

C. Jack Ramsay

D. K.C. Jones

61. Playing in Denver for coach Doug Moe during the 1980s, this player set 31 Nuggets all-time records in a ten-year stretch.

A. Dan Issel

B. Kiki Vandeweghe

C. Alex English

D. Fat Lever

62. He excelled as point guard at UCLA, compiling a 78-11 three-year record there. He later teamed with Jerry West and Wilt Chamberlain with the Lakers, once winning 33 games in a row.

    A. Mike Warren

    B. Henry Bibby

    C. Gail Goodrich

    D. John Vallely

63. He led Duke to two national championships and later was a standout forward for the Detroit Pistons, Orlando Magic, and Phoenix Suns.

    A. Grant Hill

    B. Shawn Marion

    C. Horace Grant

    D. Richard Hamilton

64. A star for the Original Celtics, he also coached at City College of New York for 33 seasons.

    A. Joe Lapchick

    B. Dick Bavetta

    C. Nat Holman

    D. Bud Foster

65. He became one of the early NBA's most prolific scorers, leading the league in scoring in 1953, 1954, and 1955.

    A. Neil Johnston

    B. George Mikan

    C. Vern Mikkelsen

    D. Bill Sharman

66. After starring at St. Johns, he played 16 seasons with the Golden State Warriors and Indiana Pacers, scoring more than 17,000 points and earning All-NBA honors four times.

A. Reggie Miller

B. Chris Mullin

C. Mitch Richmond

D. Al Attles

67. After coaching at Iowa, he moved on to Arizona, turning it into a perennial national title contender, including winning the NCAA championship in 1997.

A. Ben Lindsey

B. Lute Olsen

C. Sean Miller

D. Mike Bibby

68. This UCLA and Los Angeles Lakers great was known as "Silk."

A. Jamal Wilkes

B. Gail Goodrich

C. Walt Hazzard

D. Kareem Abdul Jabbar

69. He was the first coach in history to win both an NBA and ABA championship.

A. Doug Moe

B. Larry Brown

C. Red Auerbach

D. Alex Hannum

70. There are two men's Olympic teams enshrined in the Hall of Fame. What was the first Olympic team inducted into the Hall of Fame?

A. 1956

B. 1960

C. 1972

D. 1976

71. What was the second men's Olympic team inducted?

A. 1966

B. 1980

C. 1992

D. 1996

72. After starring at LSU and with the Orlando Magic, he teamed with Kobe Bryant and Phil Jackson to win three NBA championships with the Los Angeles Lakers in three years.

A. Robert Horry

B. Penny Hardaway

C. Shaquille O'Neal

D. Bob McAdoo

73. He teamed with Michael Jordon to win six NBA championships and was named one of the 50 Greatest Players in NBA history in 1996.

A. Bob Love

B. Luke Longley

C. Scottie Pippen

D. Horace Grant

74. This eight-time All-Star with the Dallas Mavericks and Phoenix Suns, led the league in assists five times and was a two-time MVP.

A. Steve Nash

B. Kevin Johnson

C. Jason Kidd

D. Stephon Marbury

75. He holds the distinction of having coached all of the teams he played for—Atlanta Hawks, Seattle Supersonics, Cleveland Cavaliers, and Portland Trailblazers.

A. Clyde Drexler

B. Lenny Wilkens

C. Richie Guerin

D. Rick Adleman

76. He was the NBA Rookie of the Year 1956 and he broke the NBA's single-season record for rebounds with 1,256 in just his second season while playing for the Rochester Royals.

A. Connie Dierking

B. Clyde Lovellette

C. Maurice Stokes

D. Bobby Wanzer

77. Known as "the Worm," he was a great rebounder and defender and won five NBA titles with the Detroit Pistons and Chicago Bulls.

    A. Dennis Rodman

    B. Kelly Tripuka

    C. Bob Lanier

    D. Tom Boerwinkle

78. This former Kansas star won two NBA championships while playing for the Boston Celtics.

    A. JoJo White

    B. Don Chaney

    C. Paul Westphal

    D. Emmette Bryant

79. He played over 16,000 games for the Harlem Globetrotters from 1954-1978.

A. Curly Neal

B. Meadowlark Lemon

C. Goode Tatum

D. Wilt Chamberlain

80. A former sportswriter, he became a promoter for college basketball games in the 1930s and 1940s. He helped create the National Invitation Tournament (NIT) and later founded the New York Knicks.

A. Ben Kerner

B. Walter Kennedy

C. Ned Irish

D. Daniel Biasone

81. From November 21, 1965, until December 16, 2001, he announced 3,338 consecutive games for the Los Angeles Lakers.

A. Vin Scully

B. Chick Hearn

C. Al Michaels

D. Marv Albert

82. She once scored 105 points in a high school game and tallied 3,018 total career points and was a four-time All-America at USC.

A. Cheryl Miller

B. Muffet McGraw

C. Rebecca Lobo

D. Dawn Staley

83. True or False. David Stern was NBA Commissioner for 30 years.

84. One of the top outside shooters and scorers in the early days of the NBA, he teamed with Bob Davies to help the Rochester Royals win the franchise's only title in 1950-1951.

A. Red Holzman

B. Bob Cousy

C. Bobby Wanzer

D. Satch Sanders

85. He perfected the inside reverse pivot with the Seattle Supersonics and is also the only center ever to lead the league in free throw percentage.

A. Bob Rule

B. Lonnie Shelton

C. Tom Burleson

D. Jack Sikma

86. He coached DePaul for 42 seasons, from George Mikan to Mark Aguirre.

A. Ray Meyer

B. George Keogan

C. Bobby Knight

D. John Thompson

87. He coached the San Francisco Dons, led by Bill Russell, to two national championships in 1955 and 1956.

A. Phil Knight

B. Phil Woolpert

C. Cliff Wells

D. Robert "Fuzzy" Vandivier

88. True or False. Dick Motta won over 900 games as a head coach in the NBA.

89. He was the owner of the Los Angeles Lakers beginning with the Showtime teams in the 1980s.

A. Jack Kent Cooke

B. Fred Schaus

C. Jerry Buss

D. Bob Short

90. On the night Wilt Chamberlain scored 100 points, this teammate dished out 20 assists.

A. Paul Arizin

B. Guy Rodgers

C. Al Attles

D. Tom Meschery

91. He was the first coach of the Minneapolis Lakers.

A. John Kundla

B. Pat Riley

C. George Mikan

D. Jim Pollard

92. He was co-founder and the original president of the Boston Celtics.

A. Ted Williams

B. Walter Brown

C. Red Auerbach

D. Dave Gavitt

93. College coach Bill Self coached at three other schools before landing at Kansas in 2003. What school did he NOT coach for?

A. Oral Roberts

B. Tulsa

C. Illinois

D. Minnesota

94. This center led St. Bonaventure to the Final Four in 1970, and had a stellar 14-year career with the Detroit Pistons and Milwaukee Bucks.

    A. Joe Caldwell

    B. Walt Bellamy

    C. Bob Lanier

    D. Jack Sikma

95. This Hall of Famer was a great player in his own right with the Rochester/Cincinnati Royals. However, he also became the legal guardian of paralyzed teammate Maurice Stokes and helped care for him for the remainder of his life.

    A. Adrian Smith

    B. John Tresvant

    C. Jack Twyman

D. Flynn Robinson

96. Rod Thorn's career in the NBA spanned 50 years. During that span, he held all but one of these positions.

A. Player

B. Coach

C. General Manager

D. Referee

97. Playing alongside Larry Bird with the Celtics, this strong forward was the first player in NBA history to shoot 60% from the floor and 80% from the free throw line in a season.

A. Cornbread Maxwell

B. Kevin McHale

C. John Havlicek

D. Satch Sanders

98. He was the Phoenix Suns leading scorer when he reached the NBA Finals in 1976, and was the head coach when they reached the Finals again in 1993.

A. Paul Wetzel

B. Pat Riley

C. Paul Westphal

D. Gar Heard

99. Who was the head coach of the Phoenix Suns when they played the Boston Celtics in the 1976 NBA Finals?

A. John MacLeod

B. Al Bianchi

C. Cotton Fitzsimmons

D. Jerry Colangelo

100. This point guard for the Illinois "Whiz Kids" of the early 1940s, later played for four NBA teams, leading the league in assists twice.

A. Andy Philip

B. Norm Van Lier

C. Bob Feerick

D. Buddy Jeanette

Answers

1. The Basketball Hall of Fame is named after James Naismith, the inventor of the game.

2. The Hall of Fame is located in Springfield Massachusetts, where Naismith invented basketball.

3. In 1921, Chuck Taylor convinced the shoemaker Converse to create a shoe just for basketball. The company did and in 1932 put Taylor's name on its shoe.

4. The first basketball Hall of Fame class was inducted in 1959.

5. The Original Celtics were part of the first Hal of Fame class in 1959.

6. George Mikan, who had a stellar college career with DePaul and pro career with the Minneapolis Lakers.

7. John Wooden is in the Hall of Fame as both a player and a coach.

8. John "Cat" Thompson led the Montana State Golden Bobcats to a 102-11 record during his collegiate days.

9. Chuck Cooper was drafted by the Boston Celtics in 1950.

10. Julius Erving began his career in the ABA before moving to the NBA following the NBA-ABA merger.

11. The 1966 national champion Texas Western team was inducted into the Hall of Fame for, not only beating Kentucky in the national championship game, but also because it broke barriers by being the first school to start an all-black team in that game.

12. Maurice Podoloff simultaneously held the positions of commissioner of the National Basketball Association and president of the American Hockey League.

13. Frank Ramsey starred at Kentucky and with the Boston Celtics.

14. Rudy Tomjanovich played 11 seasons with the Rockets, averaging over 17 points per game during his playing career. He later coached the Rockets for 12 seasons, winning two championships.

15. Chet "The Jet" Walker averaged over 18 points per game during his career.

16. Bob Pettit won Rookie of the Year honors as well as being named MVP twice.

17. Bill Walton was UCLA's center and star during their 88-game winning streak and made a remarkable 21 of 22 shots against Memphis in the 1973 national championship game.

18. David Robinson enjoyed a great career with the San Antonio Spurs in the NBA following his collegiate career at Navy.

19. Bill Russell won his second national championship with San Francisco, then led the Olympic team to a gold medal, followed by his first NBA championship as a rookie with the Boston Celtics, all within a 13-month period.

20. Nancy Lieberman starred at Old Dominion University, averaging over 18 points per game in her four-year career.

21. Gus Johnson played for the Baltimore Bullets from 1963-1972, as well as brief stints with the Phoenix Suns and Indiana Pacers (ABA), averaging over 16 points and 12 rebounds per game for his career.

22. Oscar Robertson was known as the "Big O." He led Cincinnati University to two Final Fours and had a Hall of Fame career with the Cincinnati Royals and Milwaukee Bucks in the NBA.

23. John Havlicek won an NCAA title with Ohio State in 1960 and was a main cog in eight Boston Celtics titles.

24. Clair Bee coached at Long Island University from 1931-1951, as well as three years at Rider before that, comping a lifetime winning percentage of .824.

25. Jason Kidd is second all-time in assists with 12,091.

26. Tamika Catchings was a four-time Olympic gold medalist, as well as a star at Tennessee and in the WNBA. She is the daughter of former NBA player Harvey Catchings.

27. George Yardley starred at Stanford and played seven season in the NBA, scoring 2,001 points in the 1957-1958 season with the Detroit Pistons.

28. Roger Brown averaged 17.4 points per game over his ABA career.

29. True. Magic Johnson is the Lakers all-time assist leader with 10,141.

30. Former Georgetown center Dikembe Mutombo played for six teams over his 18-year career.

31. Connie Hawkins played two years in the ABA before joining the Phoenix Suns.

32. "Easy" Ed Macauley played for the St. Louis Bombers, Boston Celtics, and St. Louis Hawks during his NBA career.

33. Following his career at Niagara, the diminutive Calvin Murphy averaged 17.9 points per game over his career with the San Diego/Houston Rockets.

34. Spencer Haywood left the University of Detroit early to join the ABA, at a time when the NBA required collegiate players to wait until their class had completed four years of college in order to be eligible to be drafted.

35. Willis Reed was the NBA Finals MVP in 1970 and 1973 for the New York Knicks.

36. Dean Smith would incorporate the four-corners offense to protect a lead late in games.

37. Richie Guerin average 17.3 points per game over his 13-year career with the New York Knicks and St. Louis/Atlanta Hawks. He coached the Hawks for eight seasons, most of those as player-coach.

38. Moses Malone joined to the Utah Stars of the ABA directly out of high school in 1974-1975, averaging 18.8 points per game and 14.6 rebounds per game in his first season.

39. Lisa Leslie played 12 seasons with the Los Angeles Sparks in the WNBA, winning two titles and three MVP awards.

40. Don Nelson played in 1,053 regular season games and 150 playoff games. He coached in 2,398 regular season games and 166 playoff games.

41. James Worthy starred at North Carolina with Michael Jordon and then won three NBA championships teaming with Magic Johnson and the Lakers.

42. Pete Newell won the NIT while coaching San Francisco in 1948-1949, the NCAA championship while at California in 1958-1959, and an Olympic gold medal in 1960.

43. John Thompson played two seasons with the Boston Celtics from 1964-1966 and later coached Georgetown for 27 years.

44. At 28, Jerry Colangelo became the youngest general manager in professional sports in 1968 with the Phoenix Suns.

45. Fred Zollner owned the Pistons, first in Fort Wayne and later in Detroit, from 1941-1974.

46. Bob Davies was known as eh "Harrisburg Houdini."

47. Charles "Lefty" Driesell coached at Davidson, Maryland, James Madison, and Georgia State.

48. Sidney Moncrief starred at Arkansas and later with the Milwaukee Bucks.

49. K.C. Jones won two NCAA championships with Bill Russell at San Francisco and then teamed with Russell for eight more NBA championships with the Boston Celtics.

50. False. Pat Summitt led the Tennessee Lady Vols to 18 Final Four appearances, still an NCAA record.

51. Bobby Jones was named to the All-Defensive team multiple times while playing with the Denver Nuggets and Philadelphia 76ers.

52. Michael Jordon won three consecutive NBA titles with the Chicago Bulls. Then he tried his hand at minor league baseball for two years before returning to lead the Bulls to three more championships.

53. Kobe Bryant is the Los Angeles Lakers all-time leading scorer with 33,643 points.

54. Walt Bellamy was Rookie of the Year in 1961-1962, while playing for the Chicago Packers.

55. Ann Meyers-Drysdale was named to four consecutive All-America teams while at UCLA.

56. Bobby Knight coached Indiana and later Texas Tech.

57. Pat Riley became one of the winningest coaches in NBA history with the Lakers, the Knicks, and the Heat.

58. Dave Cowens exemplified hustle during his playing career, while winning two championships with the Celtics.

59. Dolph Schayes scored over 19,000 points during his 16-year career.

60. Jack Ramsey coached four teams and won an NBA championship while coaching the Portland Trailblazers in 1976-1977.

61. Alex English set 31 team records while playing for the Nuggets, including a high scoring average of 25.9 points per game during his time with Denver.

62. Gail Goodrich won two NCAA championships with UCLA and later won an NBA championship with the Lakers in 1971-1972.

63. Grant Hill excelled while at Duke and was a seven-time All-Star in the NBA.

64. Nat Homan was one of the stars of the Original Celtics and coached CCNY for 33 years, leading them to the NIT championship and NCAA championship in 1948-1950.

65. Neil Johnston played eight seasons in the NBA, all for the Philadelphia Warriors, averaging 19.4 point per game for his career.

66. Chris Mullin had a standout career at St. Johns, followed by a career in the NBA that included five All-Star appearances.

67. Lute Olsen arrived at Arizona after the school had won only four games the previous season. He proceeded to turn the program into a regular in the NCAA tournament that included four Final Four appearances and one national championship.

68. Jamel Wilkes, originally known as Keith, won two NCAA championships with UCLA and four NBA championships, one with the Golden State Warriors and three with the Los Angeles Lakers.

69. Alex Hannum coached the St. Louis Hawks and the Philadelphia 76ers to NBA championships and later led the Oakland Oaks to an ABA title.

70. The 1960 gold medal-winning Olympic team that included Jerry West, Oscar Robertson, and Jerry Lucas is considered to be the greatest amateur team ever assembled and won by an average margin of over 40 points

71. The 1992 "Dream Team," featuring Michael Jordon, Magic Johnson, Larry Bird, and Charles Barkley, was the

first Olympic team to include professional players. The team cruised to a gold medal, winning by an average margin of over 44 points per game.

72. Shaquille O'Neal played 19 seasons in the NBA, winning four titles and one MVP award.

73. Scotty Pippen won six titles with the Bulls during his NBA career.

74. Point Guard had two stints with the Phoenix Suns and one with the Dallas Mavericks, winning two MVP awards while a member of the Suns.

75. Lenny Wilkens eventually coached for all of the four teams he played with, including stints as player-coach with the Seattle Supersonics and Portland Trailblazers.

76. Maurice Stokes had a great start to his NBA career before a head injury in his third season that ultimately left him paralyzed, cutting short his promising career.

77. Dennis Rodman led the league in rebounding seven times during his 14-year career.

78. Jo Jo White won NBA titles with the Celtics in 1973-1974 and 1975-1976.

79. In addition to playing over 16,000 games for the Globetrotters, Meadowlark Lemon also played in 7,500 consecutive games.

80. Ned Irish helped created the NIT and served as President of the New York Knicks from 1946-1974.

81. The voice of the Los Angeles Lakers, Chick Hearn broadcast Lakers games for over 36 years.

82. Cheryl Miller once scored 105 points in a high school game while playing for Riverside Polytechnic High School in California. She later starred at USC, winning the Naismith Player of the Year award three times.

83. True. David Stern spent 30 years as NBA commissioner.

84. Bobby Wanzer was a great shooter and all-around player. He was a five-time All-Star and was one of the first NBA players to shoot over 90% from the free throw line.

85. Jack Sikma's patented inside revers pivot helped him become an All-Star with the Seattle Supersonics. He led the NBA in free throw percentage in 1987-1988 while with the Milwaukee Bucks, shooting at a .922 clip.

86. Rey Meyer was the long-time coach of DePaul, leading them to 13 NCAA tournaments and two Final Fours.

87. Phil Woolpert coached for nine seasons at San Francisco, winning two NCAA titles in 1954-1955 and 1955-1956.

88. True. Dick Motta won 935 games over 25 seasons as a head coach in the NBA.

89. Jerry Buss owned the Los Angeles Lakers from 1979 until his death in 2013.

90. Point Guard Guy Rodgers dished out 20 assists on the night Wilt Chamberlain scored 100 points. He was a four-time All-Star over his twelve-year career, leading the NBA in assists twice.

91. John Kundla was the first coach of the Minneapolis Lakers, leading them to five titles in the first six years.

92. Walter Brown co-founded the Boston Celtics and was president of the team during its first seven NBA titles.

93. Bill Self never coached at Minnesota.

94. Following his collegiate career, Bob Lanier was an eight-time All-Star during his NBA career.

95. Jack Twyman, a Cincinnati Royals teammate of Maurice Stokes, averaged 19.2 points per game during his 11-year career, while also taking on the responsibility of caring for Stokes as his legal guardian.

96. Rod Thorn was a player, coach, general manager, and even served in the league office, but he was never a referee.

97. Kevin McHale won three NBA titles while playing with Larry Bird and the Celtics. In 1986-1987, he shot .604 from the field and .836 from the free throw line.

98. Paul Westphal averaged a team-leading 20.5 points per game in his first year as a player for the Phoenix Suns in 1975-1976 and coached them to a 62-20 record and an appearance in the NBA Finals in his first year as the Suns head coach in 1992-1993.

99. John McLeod was head coach of the Phoenix Suns when they played in the 1975-1976 NBA Finals.

100. Andy Philip was a seven-time All-Star and was the NBA first player to dish out 500 assists in one season.

Acknowledgements

This is a special thanks to the following history lovers who have taken time out of their busy schedule to be part of History Compacted Launch Team. Thank you all so much for all the feedbacks and support. Let's continue our journey to simplify the stories of history!

Anthony Rodriguez, Axel Andersen, Casey Bates, Karol Pietka, Charisse Peeler, Christian Loucq, CLARA PRATT, Dave Kaiser, Don Voorhees, Ellen Martin, Adas, Frankline, Victor Harris, Hans G. Wenze, Janalyn Prude Bergeron, JANEL IVERSON, Kim Lyon, Kevin Gilhooly, Maryann Mahan, Matthew Peters, Mike Blume, Amanda Kliebert, Daphne Palmer, Rick Conley, Ricky Burk, Ronald Macaulay, Steve Thomson, Holli-Marie Taylor, Kris Thorstenson, Judy Kirkbride, Ray Workman, Bill Anderson, Warren Moretz, Yaen. Vered

About History Compacted

Here in History Compacted, we see history as a large collection of stories. Each of these amazing stories of the past can help spark ideas for the future. However, history is often proceeded as boring and incomprehensible. That is why it is our mission to simplify the fascinating stories of history.

Visit Us At: www.historycompacted.com

Dark Minds In History

For updates about new releases, as well as exclusive promotions, sign up for our newsletter and you can also receive a free book today. Thank you and see you soon.

Sign up here: https://freebook.historycompacted.com/

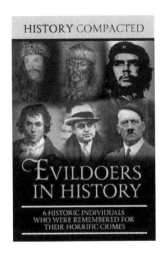

Evildoers in History: 6 Historic Individuals Remembered For Their Horrific Crimes is a book that explores the stories of six infamous criminals in history, these evildoers were not remembered by their countless murders but by the brutality with which they took the lives of their victims. There is no other term to describe them but ruthless, as you will soon find out.

Prepare yourself, the gruesome part of history is not for everyone...

Made in United States
Troutdale, OR
12/19/2023

16123348R00235